Savouring Tradition

A Journey into Classic Indian Cookery

By Steven Heap

ISBN: 9798396974968

Preface

Welcome to the enchanting world of Indian cuisine! This recipe book is a tribute to the timeless and diverse culinary traditions that have shaped the rich tapestry of Indian cooking. Within these pages, you will embark on a gastronomic journey through the vibrant landscapes and food heritage of this extraordinary land.

Indian cuisine is a harmonious symphony of flavours, colours, and aromas, influenced by centuries of invasions, trade routes, and regional diversity. It is a testament to the ingenuity and creativity of the Indian people, who have perfected the art of transforming humble ingredients into extraordinary dishes that tantalize the taste buds and nourish the soul.

Whether you are a seasoned chef, an adventurous food enthusiast, or a curious novice, this book aims to be your trusted companion in unravelling the secrets of Indian cooking. The recipes have been thoughtfully selected to cater to a wide range of tastes and dietary preferences,

But this book is more than just a collection of recipes; it is a gateway to understanding the heart and soul of Indian culture. It is an invitation to connect with the people, customs, and stories that have shaped this magnificent cuisine.

So, tie on your apron, sharpen your knives, and prepare to embark on a culinary adventure that will awaken your senses and transport you to the vibrant world of Indian flavours. May this book inspire you to explore, create, and savour the magic of Indian cuisine. Enjoy the journey!

Happy Cooking!

Index

RICE

Plain Basmati Rice 70
Pilau 72
Veg Pilau 74
Jeera Rice 76

BIRYANI

Veg Biryani 78
Lamb Biryani 80
Bombay Biryani 82
Hydrabadi Biryani 86
Prawn Biryani 88
Fish Biryani 90

SIDE DISHES

Tadka Dhal 94
Chana Masala 96
Saag Aloo 98
Aloo Gobi 100
Palak Paneer 10
Bombay Potatoes 104
Dhal Makhani 106

CHUTNEYS & PICKLES

Coriander Chutney 110
Tamarind Chutney 111
Garlic Chutney 113
Date Chutney 114
Lime Pickle 116
Mango Pickle 117
Kachumba Salad 119
Raita 120

DESSERTS

Dhokla 122
Gulab Jamun 124
Ras Malai 126
Coconut Barfi 128
Rice Pudding 130
Kulfi 132
Halwa 134

Starters

Garam Masala

Let's start by making your own Garam masala which is a blend of ground spices commonly used in Indian cuisine. It adds a warm and aromatic flavour to dishes.

Ingredients

- 2 tablespoons whole coriander seeds
- 1 tablespoon cumin seeds
- 1 tablespoon black peppercorns
- 1 tablespoon green cardamom pods
- 1 cinnamon stick (about 2 inches)
- 1 teaspoon whole cloves
- 1 teaspoon fennel seeds
- 1 teaspoon black cumin seeds (optional)
- 1 teaspoon ground nutmeg (or grated nutmeg)
- 1 teaspoon ground ginger
- 1 teaspoon turmeric powder (optional)

Instructions

1. Heat a dry skillet or pan over medium heat.
2. Add the coriander seeds, cumin seeds, black peppercorns, green cardamom pods, cinnamon stick, cloves, fennel seeds, and black cumin seeds (if using) to the pan.
3. Toast the spices for about 2-3 minutes, stirring occasionally, until they become fragrant and slightly darker in colour. Be careful not to burn them.
4. Remove the pan from heat and let the toasted spices cool completely.
5. Transfer the cooled spices to a spice grinder or mortar and pestle. Grind them into a fine powder.
6. Add the ground nutmeg, ground ginger, and turmeric powder (if using) to the ground spice mixture. Mix well to combine all the spices evenly.

7. Store the homemade garam masala in an airtight container in a cool, dark place. It will stay fresh for several months.

Chicken Tikka

Chicken tikka is a popular Indian dish known for its succulent and flavourful grilled chicken pieces.

Ingredients

- 500 grams boneless chicken, cut into bite-sized pieces
- 1/2 cup plain yogurt
- 2 tablespoons lemon juice
- 2 tablespoons ginger-garlic paste
- 1 tablespoon tikka masala or tandoori masala powder
- 1 teaspoon turmeric powder
- 1 teaspoon cumin powder
- 1 teaspoon coriander powder
- 1/2 teaspoon red chilli powder (adjust according to spice preference)
- 1/2 teaspoon garam masala powder
- 2 tablespoons oil
- Salt to taste
- Skewers for grilling
- Chopped coriander and lemon wedges for garnish

Instructions

1. In a bowl, combine the yogurt, lemon juice, ginger-garlic paste, tikka masala or tandoori masala powder, turmeric powder, cumin powder, coriander powder, red chilli powder, garam masala powder, oil, and salt. Mix well to form a smooth marinade.
2. Add the chicken pieces to the marinade and mix until each piece is coated evenly. Make sure the chicken is well-marinated and refrigerate for at least 2 hours, or overnight for the best flavour.
3. If using wooden skewers, soak them in water for 30 minutes to prevent burning.
4. Preheat your grill to medium-high heat or preheat your oven to the highest temperature for broiling.

5. Thread the marinated chicken pieces onto the skewers, shaking off any excess marinade.
6. If using a grill, lightly oil the grates to prevent sticking. Place the skewers on the grill and cook for about 8-10 minutes per side, or until the chicken is cooked through and has a slight char. If using an oven, place the skewers on a baking sheet lined with aluminium foil and placed on the top rack. Broil for about 10-12 minutes, turning the skewers halfway through cooking, until the chicken is cooked through and nicely browned.
7. Remove the chicken tikka skewers from the grill or oven and let them rest for a few minutes.
8. Garnish with chopped coriander and serve hot with lemon wedges on the side.

Chicken tikka is a versatile dish that can be enjoyed on its own as an appetizer or served with naan bread, rice, or salad as a main course. It is best served hot and pairs well with mint chutney or yogurt dip.

Paneer Tikka

Paneer tikka is a popular Indian appetizer made with marinated and grilled cubes of paneer (Indian cottage cheese) along with vegetables. It is a flavourful and delicious dish that can be enjoyed as a starter or as a part of a main course.

Ingredients

- 250 grams paneer, cut into cubes
- 1 medium-sized bell pepper (capsicum), cut into cubes
- 1 medium-sized onion, cut into cubes
- 1 cup plain yogurt (hung curd)
- 1 tablespoon ginger-garlic paste
- 1 tablespoon lemon juice
- 1 tablespoon tikka masala or tandoori masala powder
- 1 teaspoon turmeric powder
- 1 teaspoon cumin powder
- 1 teaspoon coriander powder
- 1/2 teaspoon red chilli powder (adjust according to spice preference)
- 1/2 teaspoon garam masala powder
- 2 tablespoons oil
- Salt to taste
- Skewers for grilling
- Chopped coriander for garnish
- Lemon wedges for serving

Instructions

1. In a bowl, combine the hung curd, ginger-garlic paste, lemon juice, tikka masala or tandoori masala powder, turmeric powder, cumin powder, coriander powder, red chilli powder, garam masala powder, oil, and salt. Mix well to form a smooth marinade.
2. Add the paneer cubes, bell pepper, and onion cubes to the marinade. Gently toss to coat the paneer and vegetables with the marinade. Make sure all the pieces are well-coated. Let the mixture

marinate in the refrigerator for at least 1-2 hours, or overnight for the best flavour.

3. If using wooden skewers, soak them in water for 30 minutes to prevent burning.
4. Preheat your grill to medium-high heat or preheat your oven to the highest temperature for broiling.
5. Thread the marinated paneer cubes, bell pepper, and onion onto the skewers, alternating between them.
6. If using a grill, lightly oil the grates to prevent sticking. Place the skewers on the grill and cook for about 8-10 minutes, turning the skewers occasionally, until the paneer and vegetables are lightly charred and cooked through. If using an oven, place the skewers on a baking sheet lined with aluminium foil and placed on the top rack. Broil for about 10-12 minutes, turning the skewers halfway through cooking, until the paneer and vegetables are lightly charred and cooked through.
7. Remove the paneer tikka skewers from the grill or oven and let them rest for a few minutes.
8. Garnish with chopped coriander and serve hot with lemon wedges on the side.

Kebab

One of the best Indian kebab recipes is the Seekh Kebab, a popular and flavourful kebab made with minced meat and a blend of aromatic spices.

Ingredients

- 500 grams minced meat (chicken, lamb, or beef)
- 1 medium-sized onion, finely chopped
- 2 tablespoons ginger-garlic paste
- 2 tablespoons finely chopped coriander
- 1 tablespoon finely chopped mint leaves
- 1 tablespoon gram flour (besan)
- 1 teaspoon red chilli powder
- 1 teaspoon coriander powder
- 1 teaspoon cumin powder
- 1/2 teaspoon garam masala powder
- 1/2 teaspoon turmeric powder
- 1/2 teaspoon black pepper powder
- 1/2 teaspoon salt (adjust to taste)
- 1 tablespoon lemon juice
- 2 tablespoons oil
- Skewers for grilling

Instructions

1. In a large mixing bowl, combine the minced meat, chopped onion, ginger-garlic paste, chopped coriander, chopped mint leaves, gram flour, red chilli powder, coriander powder, cumin powder, garam masala powder, turmeric powder, black pepper powder, salt, lemon juice, and oil. Mix well to combine all the ingredients.
2. Cover the bowl with plastic wrap or a lid and let the mixture marinate in the refrigerator for at least 1-2 hours to allow the flavours to meld together.
3. If using wooden skewers, soak them in water for 30 minutes to prevent burning.

4. Preheat your grill to medium-high heat or preheat your oven to the highest temperature for broiling.
5. Take a handful of the marinated meat mixture and shape it around a skewer, pressing and moulding it to form a cylindrical shape. Repeat the process with the remaining meat mixture and skewers.
6. If using a grill, lightly oil the grates to prevent sticking. Place the skewers on the grill and cook for about 8-10 minutes, turning occasionally, until the kebabs are cooked through and have a nice char on the outside. If using an oven, place the skewers on a baking sheet lined with aluminium foil and placed on the top rack. Broil for about 10-12 minutes, turning the skewers halfway through cooking, until the kebabs are cooked through and have a nice char on the outside.
7. Remove the Seekh Kebabs from the grill or oven and let them rest for a few minutes.
8. Serve the kebabs hot with mint chutney, tamarind chutney, or yogurt dip. You can also squeeze some lemon juice over the kebabs for an extra burst of flavour.

Kebabs are perfect as appetizers or as a main course served with naan bread, rice, or salad.

Onion Bhaji

Onion bhajis, also known as onion pakoras, are crispy and flavourful Indian fritters made with a batter of gram flour (besan) and onions. They make a perfect appetizer or snack.

Ingredients

- 2 medium-sized onions, thinly sliced
- 1 cup gram flour (besan)
- 2 tablespoons rice flour (optional, for extra crispiness)
- 1 teaspoon cumin seeds
- 1/2 teaspoon turmeric powder
- 1/2 teaspoon red chilli powder (adjust according to spice preference)
- 1/2 teaspoon garam masala powder
- 1/2 teaspoon baking soda
- Salt to taste
- Water, as needed
- Oil for deep frying
- Chopped coriander for garnish
- Lemon wedges for serving

Instructions

1. In a large mixing bowl, combine the gram flour, rice flour (if using), cumin seeds, turmeric powder, red chilli powder, garam masala powder, baking soda, and salt. Mix well to combine the dry ingredients.
2. Add the thinly sliced onions to the dry ingredient mixture and mix well to coat the onions evenly. The moisture from the onions will help bind the mixture together. If needed, add a little water at a time to form a thick batter. The batter should be thick enough to coat the onions, but not too runny.
3. Heat oil in a deep pan or kadai for deep frying. The oil should be at medium-high heat.

4. Take small portions of the onion batter using your fingers or a spoon and drop them gently into the hot oil. Fry in batches, making sure not to overcrowd the pan.
5. Fry the onion bhajis until they turn golden brown and crispy, turning them occasionally for even cooking. This usually takes about 4-5 minutes per batch.
6. Once done, remove the fried onion bhajis using a slotted spoon and place them on a paper towel-lined plate to drain excess oil.
7. Repeat the frying process with the remaining batter and onions until all the bhajis are fried.
8. Garnish the onion bhajis with chopped coriander.
9. Serve the hot and crispy onion bhajis with mint chutney, tamarind chutney, or ketchup. Squeeze some lemon juice over the bhajis for an extra tangy flavour.

Tandoori Chicken

Tandoori chicken is a popular Indian dish known for its vibrant red colour and smoky flavour. Traditionally, it is cooked in a tandoor (clay oven), but you can still achieve similar results without a tandoor.

Ingredients

- 4 chicken drumsticks or bone-in chicken pieces
- 1/2 cup plain yogurt
- 2 tablespoons lemon juice
- 2 tablespoons vegetable oil
- 2 teaspoons ginger-garlic paste
- 2 teaspoons tandoori masala (available in stores or homemade)
- 1 teaspoon paprika (for colour)
- 1 teaspoon ground cumin
- 1 teaspoon ground coriander
- 1/2 teaspoon turmeric powder
- 1/2 teaspoon red chilli powder (adjust according to spice preference)
- Salt to taste
- Fresh coriander leaves for garnish
- Lemon wedges for serving

Instructions

1. In a mixing bowl, combine the yogurt, lemon juice, vegetable oil, ginger-garlic paste, tandoori masala, paprika, ground cumin, ground coriander, turmeric powder, red chilli powder, and salt. Mix well to form a smooth marinade.
2. Add the chicken pieces to the marinade and coat them evenly with the mixture. Make sure the chicken is well coated with the marinade.
3. Cover the bowl and refrigerate the chicken for at least 2 hours, or preferably overnight, to allow the flavours to develop.
4. Preheat a grill or stovetop pan over medium heat. If using a stovetop pan, you can grease it lightly with oil to prevent sticking.

5. Place the marinated chicken pieces on the grill or pan. Cook them for about 6-8 minutes on each side, or until they are cooked through and have a slightly charred appearance. You can brush the chicken with a little oil while cooking to keep it moist.
6. Once cooked, transfer the tandoori chicken to a serving plate.
7. Garnish with fresh coriander leaves and serve hot with lemon wedges on the side.

Veg Samosa

Veg Samosas are delicious and popular Indian snacks that are enjoyed all over the world. These crispy, triangular pastries are filled with a savoury mixture of vegetables and spices.

For the dough

- 2 cups all-purpose flour
- 1/2 teaspoon salt
- 1/4 cup oil
- Water, as needed

Instructions

1. In a mixing bowl, combine the all-purpose flour and salt. Mix well.
2. Add the oil to the flour mixture and rub it into the flour using your fingertips until it resembles breadcrumbs.
3. Gradually add water, a little at a time, and knead to form a smooth and firm dough.
4. Cover the dough with a damp cloth and let it rest for at least 30 minutes.

For the filling

- 2 medium-sized potatoes, boiled and mashed
- 1/2 cup green peas, boiled
- 1/2 cup finely chopped carrots
- 1/2 cup finely chopped onions
- 2 green chillies, finely chopped (adjust to taste)
- 1 teaspoon ginger-garlic paste
- 1/2 teaspoon cumin seeds
- 1/2 teaspoon coriander powder
- 1/2 teaspoon garam masala
- 1/2 teaspoon red chilli powder (adjust to taste)
- 1 tablespoon oil
- Salt to taste

- Fresh coriander leaves, finely chopped
- Oil for deep frying

Instructions

1. Heat oil in a pan over medium heat. Add the cumin seeds and let them splutter.
2. Add the finely chopped onions and sauté until they turn translucent.
3. Add the ginger-garlic paste and green chillies to the pan. Cook for a minute until the raw smell disappears.
4. Add the finely chopped carrots and boiled green peas. Sauté for a few minutes until the vegetables are slightly cooked.
5. Stir in the coriander powder, garam masala, red chilli powder, and salt. Mix well to combine the spices with the vegetables.
6. Add the mashed potatoes to the pan and mix well to coat them with the spices. Cook for a few minutes until the flavours are well combined.
7. Remove the pan from heat and garnish the filling with fresh coriander leaves. Allow the filling to cool completely.

To assemble and fry the Samosas

1. Divide the dough into small portions and roll each portion into a thin, oval-shaped sheet.
2. Cut each sheet in half to form two semi-circles.
3. Take one semi-circle and fold it into a cone shape, overlapping the edges and sealing them with a little water.
4. Fill the cone with a spoonful of the vegetable filling. Be careful not to overfill it.
5. Apply a little water to the edges of the cone and press to seal the samosa.
6. Repeat the process with the remaining dough and filling.
7. Heat oil in a deep pan or kadai for deep frying.
8. Once the oil is hot, carefully slide a few samosas into the hot oil and fry them until they turn golden brown and crispy.
9. Remove the fried samosas from the oil and drain them on a kitchen paper towel to remove excess oil.

Lamb Samosa

Lamb Samosas are delicious and filled with a savoury lamb mixture and deep-fried to crispy perfection.

For the dough

- 2 cups all-purpose flour
- 1/2 teaspoon salt
- 1/4 cup oil
- Water, as needed

Instructions

1. In a mixing bowl, combine the all-purpose flour and salt. Mix well.
2. Add the oil to the flour mixture and rub it into the flour using your fingertips until it resembles breadcrumbs.
3. Gradually add water, a little at a time, and knead to form a smooth and firm dough.
4. Cover the dough with a damp cloth and let it rest for at least 30 minutes.

For the filling

- 250 grams ground lamb
- 1/2 cup finely chopped onions
- 2 cloves garlic, minced
- 1-inch piece of ginger, grated
- 1 green chilli, finely chopped (adjust to taste)
- 1/2 teaspoon cumin seeds
- 1/2 teaspoon coriander powder
- 1/2 teaspoon garam masala
- 1/2 teaspoon red chilli powder (adjust to taste)
- 1 tablespoon oil
- Salt to taste
- Fresh coriander leaves, finely chopped
- Oil for deep frying

Instructions

1. Heat oil in a pan over medium heat. Add the cumin seeds and let them splutter.
2. Add the finely chopped onions and sauté until they turn translucent.
3. Add the minced garlic, grated ginger, and green chilli to the pan. Cook for a minute until the raw smell disappears.
4. Add the ground lamb to the pan and cook until it is browned and cooked through.
5. Stir in the coriander powder, garam masala, red chilli powder, and salt. Mix well to combine the spices with the lamb.
6. Cook the lamb mixture for a few more minutes until the flavours are well combined.
7. Remove the pan from heat and garnish the filling with fresh coriander leaves. Allow the filling to cool completely.

To assemble and fry the Samosas

1. Divide the dough into small portions and roll each portion into a thin, oval-shaped sheet.
2. Cut each sheet in half to form two semi-circles.
3. Take one semi-circle and fold it into a cone shape, overlapping the edges and sealing them with a little water.
4. Fill the cone with a spoonful of the lamb filling. Be careful not to overfill it.
5. Apply a little water to the edges of the cone and press to seal the samosa.
6. Repeat the process with the remaining dough and filling.
7. Heat oil in a deep pan or kadai for deep frying.
8. Once the oil is hot, carefully slide a few samosas into the hot oil and fry them until they turn golden brown and crispy.
9. Remove the fried samosas from the oil and drain them on a kitchen paper towel to remove excess oil.
10. Repeat the frying process with the remaining samosas.

Serve the crispy Lamb Samosas hot with mint chutney or tamarind chutney. They make for a delightful appetizer or snack.

Main Dishes

Chicken Tikka Masala

Chicken Tikka Masala is a popular and flavourful dish that combines marinated and grilled chicken pieces with a creamy and spices tomato based sauce.

Ingredients

- 500g boneless chicken, cut into bite-sized pieces
- 2 tablespoons vegetable oil
- 1 large onion, finely chopped
- 4 cloves of garlic, minced
- 1-inch piece of ginger, grated
- 2 teaspoons ground cumin
- 2 teaspoons ground coriander
- 1 teaspoon turmeric powder
- 1 teaspoon paprika
- 1 teaspoon garam masala
- 1 teaspoon chilli powder (adjust according to spice preference)
- 200g tomato puree
- 200ml heavy cream
- Salt to taste
- Fresh coriander leaves, chopped (for garnish)

Marinade

- 200g plain yogurt
- 2 tablespoons lemon juice
- 1 teaspoon ground cumin
- 1 teaspoon ground coriander
- 1 teaspoon paprika
- 1 teaspoon turmeric powder
- 1 teaspoon garam masala
- Salt to taste

Instructions

1. In a bowl, combine all the marinade ingredients and mix well. Add the chicken pieces, ensuring they are well coated. Marinate for at least 2 hours or overnight in the refrigerator.
2. Preheat the oven to 200°C (400°F). Place the marinated chicken on a baking sheet and cook for 15-20 minutes or until the chicken is cooked through and slightly charred. Set aside.
3. In a large pan, heat the vegetable oil over medium heat. Add the chopped onions and sauté until golden brown.
4. Add the minced garlic and grated ginger to the pan and cook for another minute, stirring constantly.
5. Reduce the heat to low and add the ground cumin, ground coriander, turmeric powder, paprika, garam masala, and chilli powder. Stir well to combine and cook for a couple of minutes to toast the spices.
6. Add the tomato puree to the pan and cook for about 5 minutes, stirring occasionally.
7. Stir in the cooked chicken pieces, ensuring they are coated with the sauce. Cook for another 5 minutes to allow the flavours to meld together.
8. Pour in the heavy cream and stir gently to incorporate. Simmer the curry for an additional 5 minutes.
9. Taste and adjust the seasoning with salt as needed.
10. Garnish with fresh coriander leaves and serve hot with steamed rice or naan bread.

Chana Bhuture

Chana Bhature is a popular North Indian dish that consists of spicy chickpea curry (chana) served with deep-fried bread (bhature).

For Chana (Chickpea Curry)

Ingredients

- 1 cup dried chickpeas (chana), soaked overnight
- 2 medium-sized onions, finely chopped
- 2 tomatoes, finely chopped
- 2 green chillies, slit (adjust to taste)
- 1 tablespoon ginger-garlic paste
- 1 teaspoon cumin seeds
- 1 teaspoon turmeric powder
- 1 teaspoon red chilli powder (adjust to taste)
- 1 teaspoon garam masala
- 1 teaspoon dried mango powder (amchur)
- Salt to taste
- 2 tablespoons oil
- Fresh coriander leaves, for garnish

Instructions

1. Rinse the soaked chickpeas and transfer them to a pressure cooker. Add enough water to cover the chickpeas and pressure cook for about 15-20 minutes or until they are soft and cooked through. Drain and set aside.
2. Heat oil in a pan over medium heat. Add the cumin seeds and let them splutter.
3. Add the chopped onions to the pan and sauté until they turn golden brown.
4. Add the ginger-garlic paste and slit green chillies to the pan. Cook for a minute until the raw smell disappears.
5. Add the chopped tomatoes to the pan and cook until they become soft and mushy.

6. Stir in the turmeric powder, red chilli powder, garam masala, and dried mango powder. Mix well to combine the spices with the tomato-onion mixture.
7. Add the cooked chickpeas to the pan and mix well to coat them with the spices. Cook for a few minutes until the flavours are well combined.
8. Add salt to taste and adjust the consistency by adding water if needed. Simmer the chana on low heat for about 10-15 minutes to allow the flavours to develop.
9. Garnish the Chana with fresh coriander leaves.

For Bhature (Deep-fried Bread)

* 2 cups all-purpose flour
* 1/2 cup yogurt
* 1 teaspoon baking powder
* 1/2 teaspoon baking soda
* 1 tablespoon oil
* Salt to taste
* Oil for deep frying

Instructions

1. In a mixing bowl, combine the all-purpose flour, yogurt, baking powder, baking soda, oil, and salt. Mix well to form a smooth dough. Add water if needed to achieve the right consistency. Knead the dough for a few minutes until it is soft and pliable.
2. Cover the dough with a damp cloth and let it rest for at least 2 hours to allow it to ferment.
3. After the resting period, divide the dough into small portions and roll each portion into a circular shape using a rolling pin.
4. Heat oil in a deep pan or kadai for deep frying. Once the oil is hot, carefully slide the rolled bhature into the hot oil. Gently press it with a slotted spoon to help it puff up. Fry until the bhature turn golden brown on both sides.
5. Remove the fried bhature from the oil and drain them on a kitchen paper towel to remove excess oil.

Lamb Rogan Josh

This Lamb Rogan Josh recipe showcases the aromatic blend of spices and slow-cooked tender lamb, resulting in a rich and flavourful curry. Feel free to adjust the spice levels and ingredients according to your taste preferences. Enjoy the exquisite taste of this traditional Kashmiri lamb curry!

Ingredients

- 1 kg lamb, cut into pieces
- 3 tablespoons vegetable oil
- 2 large onions, finely chopped
- 4 cloves of garlic, minced
- 1-inch piece of ginger, grated
- 2 teaspoons ground cumin
- 2 teaspoons ground coriander
- 1 teaspoon turmeric powder
- 1 teaspoon chilli powder (adjust according to spice preference)
- 1 teaspoon paprika
- 1 teaspoon garam masala
- 1 cup plain yogurt, whisked
- 2 tomatoes, chopped
- Salt to taste
- Fresh coriander leaves, chopped (for garnish)

Instructions

1. Heat the vegetable oil in a large pan over medium heat. Add the chopped onions and sauté until golden brown.
2. Add the minced garlic and grated ginger to the pan and cook for another minute, stirring constantly.
3. Reduce the heat to low and add the ground cumin, ground coriander, turmeric powder, chilli powder, paprika, and garam masala. Stir well to combine and cook for a couple of minutes to toast the spices.

4. Add the lamb pieces to the pan and cook until browned on all sides, ensuring they are coated with the spice mixture.
5. Stir in the whisked yogurt and chopped tomatoes. Mix well to combine and coat the lamb with the yogurt-tomato mixture.
6. Cover the pan and simmer the curry on low heat for about 1.5 to 2 hours, or until the lamb is tender and the flavours have developed. Stir occasionally and add a little water if needed to maintain a thick, saucy consistency.
7. Taste and adjust the seasoning with salt as needed.
8. Garnish with fresh coriander leaves and serve hot with steamed rice or naan bread.

Beef Curry

Beef curry can vary depending on personal preferences and regional tastes. However, here's a delicious and popular recipe for a flavourful beef curry.

Ingredients

- 500 grams beef, cut into cubes
- 2 onions, finely chopped
- 3 cloves of garlic, minced
- 1-inch piece of ginger, grated
- 2 tomatoes, finely chopped
- 2 tablespoons vegetable oil
- 2 teaspoons curry powder
- 1 teaspoon ground cumin
- 1 teaspoon ground coriander
- 1/2 teaspoon turmeric powder
- 1/2 teaspoon chilli powder (adjust to taste)
- 1 cinnamon stick
- 2 cardamom pods, lightly crushed
- 2 cloves
- Salt to taste
- Fresh coriander leaves, for garnish

Instructions

1. Heat the vegetable oil in a large pot or Dutch oven over medium heat. Add the onions and cook until they become golden brown and caramelized.
2. Add the minced garlic and grated ginger to the pot and sauté for another minute until fragrant.
3. Add the beef cubes to the pot and cook, stirring occasionally, until they are browned on all sides.
4. Add the chopped tomatoes to the pot and cook for a few minutes until they start to break down and release their juices.

5. In a small bowl, combine the curry powder, ground cumin, ground coriander, turmeric powder, and chilli powder. Mix well to form a spice blend.
6. Add the spice blend, cinnamon stick, cardamom pods, and cloves to the pot with the beef and tomatoes. Stir well to coat the beef with the spices.
7. Season with salt to taste and pour enough water into the pot to cover the beef. Bring the mixture to a boil, then reduce the heat to low, cover the pot, and let it simmer for about 1.5 to 2 hours until the beef is tender and the flavours have melded together.
8. Once the beef is cooked, taste the curry and adjust the seasoning if needed.
9. Garnish the beef curry with fresh coriander leaves.

Serve the flavourful beef curry with steamed rice or naan bread for a delicious and satisfying meal. Enjoy the aromatic spices and tender beef in every bite!

Pork Vindaloo

Pork Vindaloo is a popular and flavourful dish from the coastal state of Goa in India. It is known for its rich and tangy flavours.

Ingredients

- 500 grams pork, cut into cubes
- 2 onions, finely chopped
- 4 cloves of garlic, minced
- 1-inch piece of ginger, grated
- 4-5 dried red chillies (adjust to taste)
- 1 teaspoon cumin seeds
- 1 teaspoon mustard seeds
- 1 teaspoon turmeric powder
- 1 teaspoon ground coriander
- 1/2 teaspoon ground cinnamon
- 1/2 teaspoon ground cloves
- 1/2 teaspoon sugar
- 4 tablespoons vinegar
- Salt to taste
- Vegetable oil, for cooking
- Fresh coriander leaves, for garnish

Instructions

1. In a bowl, soak the dried red chillies in warm water for about 15-20 minutes until they soften. Drain the water and set aside.
2. In a blender or food processor, blend the soaked red chillies, cumin seeds, mustard seeds, ginger, and garlic to form a smooth paste. You can add a little water if needed.
3. Heat a couple of tablespoons of vegetable oil in a large pot or Dutch oven over medium heat. Add the chopped onions and cook until they turn golden brown.
4. Add the ground spice paste to the pot and cook for a few minutes until the raw smell dissipates.

5. Add the turmeric powder, ground coriander, ground cinnamon, and ground cloves to the pot. Stir well to combine the spices with the onion and spice paste mixture.
6. Add the pork cubes to the pot and mix well, ensuring that the pork is coated with the spice mixture.
7. Pour in the vinegar and sprinkle sugar over the pork. Stir well to combine.
8. Season with salt to taste and pour enough water into the pot to cover the pork. Bring the mixture to a boil, then reduce the heat to low, cover the pot, and let it simmer for about 1.5 to 2 hours until the pork is tender and the flavours have developed.
9. Once the pork is cooked, taste the vindaloo and adjust the seasoning if needed.
10. Garnish the Pork Vindaloo with fresh coriander leaves.

Serve the Pork Vindaloo with steamed rice or naan bread for a delicious and authentic Goan meal.

How to Make Paneer

Paneer is a versatile and popular Indian cheese.

Ingredients

- 2 litres whole milk
- 2-3 tablespoons lemon juice or white vinegar
- Cheesecloth or muslin cloth
- Heavy object for pressing (such as a heavy pot or book)
- Water, for rinsing the paneer

Instructions

1. Pour the milk into a large, heavy-bottomed pan and place it over medium heat. Bring the milk to a gentle boil, stirring occasionally to prevent it from scorching or forming a skin on top.
2. Once the milk starts boiling, reduce the heat to low and slowly add the lemon juice or white vinegar, stirring gently. The acid will cause the milk to curdle and separate into curds (solid) and whey (liquid).
3. Continue stirring for a minute or two until the curds fully separate from the whey. If the whey is still milky, add a little more lemon juice or vinegar and stir gently until the separation is complete.
4. Line a colander with cheesecloth or muslin cloth and place it over a large bowl or sink to collect the whey.
5. Pour the curdled milk into the lined colander, allowing the whey to drain away. Gently rinse the curds under cold water to remove any residual lemon juice or vinegar.
6. Gather the corners of the cheesecloth and gently squeeze out any excess whey from the curds.
7. Place the wrapped curds on a flat surface and shape them into a square or rectangular block.
8. Fold the cheesecloth tightly around the curds, ensuring it covers the entire block.
9. Place the wrapped paneer on a plate or tray and put a heavy object on top to press it. This helps to remove any remaining whey and shape the paneer. Leave it to press for about 1-2 hours.

10. After pressing, remove the weight and unwrap the paneer. Cut it into desired shapes or crumble it, depending on the recipe you intend to use it for. Can be stored in the refrigerator for up to 3-4 days.

Kadai Paneer

Kadai Paneer is a popular Indian dish made with paneer (Indian cottage cheese) cooked in a spicy tomato-based gravy, flavoured with a blend of aromatic spices.

Ingredients

- 250 grams paneer, cut into cubes
- 2 medium-sized onions, finely chopped
- 2 tomatoes, finely chopped
- 1 capsicum (bell pepper), thinly sliced
- 2 green chillies, slit (adjust to taste)
- 1 tablespoon ginger-garlic paste
- 1 teaspoon cumin seeds
- 1 teaspoon coriander seeds, crushed
- 1 teaspoon kasuri methi (dried fenugreek leaves)
- 1 teaspoon red chilli powder (adjust to taste)
- 1/2 teaspoon turmeric powder
- 1/2 teaspoon garam masala
- 1/4 cup fresh cream (optional)
- Salt to taste
- 2 tablespoons oil or ghee
- Fresh coriander leaves, for garnish

Instructions

1. Heat oil or ghee in a pan or kadai over medium heat. Add the cumin seeds and let them splutter.
2. Add the chopped onions to the pan and sauté until they turn golden brown.
3. Add the ginger-garlic paste and slit green chillies to the pan. Cook for a minute until the raw smell disappears.
4. Add the chopped tomatoes to the pan and cook until they become soft and mushy.

5. Stir in the crushed coriander seeds, turmeric powder, red chilli powder, and garam masala. Mix well to combine the spices with the tomato-onion mixture.
6. Add the sliced capsicum (bell pepper) to the pan and sauté for a few minutes until it is slightly cooked but still crunchy.
7. Add the paneer cubes to the pan and gently mix them with the spices and vegetables. Cook for a few minutes until the paneer is heated through.
8. Crush the kasuri methi between your palms and sprinkle it over the paneer mixture. Mix well to incorporate the flavours.
9. If desired, you can add fresh cream to the dish for added richness. Mix well and cook for another minute.
10. Taste and adjust the seasoning, adding salt as needed.
11. Garnish the Kadai Paneer with fresh coriander leaves.

Serve the flavourful Kadai Paneer hot with naan bread, roti, or rice. It makes a delightful vegetarian main course and pairs well with any Indian bread or rice dish. Enjoy the aromatic spices and tender paneer in this classic recipe!

Mixed Veg Curry

Mixed vegetable curry is a delicious and versatile dish that allows you to use a variety of vegetables and create a flavourful and nutritious meal.

Ingredients

- 2 tablespoons vegetable oil
- 1 onion, finely chopped
- 3 cloves of garlic, minced
- 1-inch piece of ginger, grated
- 1 green chilli, finely chopped (optional, adjust to taste)
- 2 tomatoes, finely chopped
- 1 teaspoon cumin seeds
- 1 teaspoon ground coriander
- 1/2 teaspoon turmeric powder
- 1/2 teaspoon red chilli powder (adjust to taste)
- 1/2 teaspoon garam masala
- Salt to taste
- 2 cups mixed vegetables (such as carrots, peas, cauliflower, bell peppers, potatoes, etc.), chopped
- 1 cup water
- Fresh coriander leaves, for garnish

Instructions

1. Heat the vegetable oil in a large pot or pan over medium heat. Add the cumin seeds and let them sizzle for a few seconds until fragrant.
2. Add the chopped onions to the pot and sauté until they turn golden brown.
3. Add the minced garlic, grated ginger, and chopped green chilli (if using) to the pot. Cook for another minute until the raw smell disappears.
4. Add the chopped tomatoes to the pot and cook for a few minutes until they become soft and mushy.

5. Stir in the ground coriander, turmeric powder, red chilli powder, garam masala, and salt. Mix well to combine the spices with the onion and tomato mixture.
6. Add the mixed vegetables to the pot and give them a good stir to coat them with the spice mixture.
7. Pour in the water and bring the mixture to a boil. Once it boils, reduce the heat to low, cover the pot, and let the vegetables simmer for about 15-20 minutes or until they are cooked through and tender.
8. Check the seasoning and adjust as needed.
9. Garnish the mixed vegetable curry with fresh coriander leaves.

Serve the delicious mixed vegetable curry with steamed rice, naan bread, or roti for a satisfying vegetarian meal.

Railway Mutton Curry

Railway mutton curry is a classic dish that originated in the kitchens of the Indian Railways during the British Raj. It is a flavourful and aromatic curry made with tender mutton (goat meat) and a blend of spices. Railway mutton curry is a delicious and comforting dish that is enjoyed by many. It carries the legacy of Indian Railways and is a true culinary delight.

Ingredients

- 500 grams mutton (goat meat), cut into pieces
- 2 onions, finely chopped
- 2 tomatoes, pureed
- 2 teaspoons ginger-garlic paste
- 2 green chillies, slit lengthwise
- 1/4 cup plain yogurt (curd)
- 2 tablespoons vegetable oil
- 1 teaspoon cumin seeds
- 2 bay leaves
- 2 cinnamon sticks
- 4-5 green cardamom pods
- 4-5 cloves
- 1 teaspoon turmeric powder
- 2 teaspoons red chilli powder (adjust according to spice preference)
- 1 tablespoon coriander powder
- 1 teaspoon garam masala powder
- Salt to taste
- Fresh coriander leaves for garnish

Instructions

1. Heat oil in a large, heavy-bottomed pan or pressure cooker over medium heat.
2. Add cumin seeds, bay leaves, cinnamon sticks, green cardamom pods, and cloves to the hot oil. Sauté for a minute until the spices release their aroma.

3. Add the finely chopped onions to the pan and sauté until they turn golden brown.
4. Add ginger-garlic paste and slit green chillies to the pan. Cook for a minute until the raw smell of ginger and garlic disappears.
5. Add the mutton pieces to the pan and cook on high heat for a few minutes until they are browned on all sides.
6. Reduce the heat to medium-low and add the tomato puree to the pan. Cook for a few minutes until the tomatoes are cooked and the oil separates from the mixture.
7. In a small bowl, whisk the yogurt with turmeric powder, red chilli powder, coriander powder, and salt. Add this yogurt mixture to the pan and mix well to coat the mutton with the spices.
8. If using a pressure cooker, add about 1/2 cup of water. Close the pressure cooker and cook for about 5-6 whistles, or until the mutton is tender. If using a regular pan, add about 1 cup of water, cover the pan with a lid, and simmer for 1-2 hours, or until the mutton is tender and the flavours are well-developed. Stir occasionally and add more water if needed to prevent the curry from drying out.
9. Once the mutton is cooked, sprinkle garam masala powder over the curry and mix well. Cook for another 2-3 minutes to allow the flavours to meld.
10. Garnish the railway mutton curry with fresh coriander leaves.
11. Serve the curry hot with steamed rice, naan bread, or roti.

Butter Chicken

Butter chicken, also known as Murgh Makhani, is indeed one of India's most iconic and beloved dishes. It is known for its rich and creamy tomato-based sauce that is flavoured with aromatic spices.

For the Marinade

- 500 grams boneless chicken, cut into bite-sized pieces
- 1/2 cup plain yogurt
- 1 tablespoon ginger-garlic paste
- 1 tablespoon lemon juice
- 1 teaspoon red chilli powder
- 1/2 teaspoon turmeric powder
- Salt to taste

For the Butter Chicken

- 2 tablespoons ghee or butter
- 1 onion, finely chopped
- 3 cloves of garlic, minced
- 1-inch piece of ginger, grated
- 2 green chillies, slit (optional, adjust to taste)
- 2 teaspoons ground coriander
- 2 teaspoons ground cumin
- 1 teaspoon Kashmiri red chilli powder (for colour, adjust to taste)
- 1 cup tomato puree
- 1/2 cup heavy cream
- 1 tablespoon honey or sugar
- Salt to taste
- Fresh coriander leaves, for garnish

Instructions

1. In a bowl, combine all the marinade ingredients - yogurt, ginger-garlic paste, lemon juice, red chilli powder, turmeric powder, and salt. Mix well. Add the chicken pieces to the marinade, making sure they are well coated. Cover the bowl and let the chicken marinate in the refrigerator for at least 1 hour, or overnight for best results.
2. Preheat the oven to 400°F (200°C). Place the marinated chicken on a baking sheet and cook in the oven for about 15-20 minutes, or until the chicken is cooked through and slightly charred. Alternatively, you can cook the chicken on a grill or stovetop using a grill pan.
3. In a large pan or skillet, heat the ghee or butter over medium heat. Add the chopped onions and sauté until they turn golden brown.
4. Add the minced garlic, grated ginger, and slit green chillies (if using) to the pan. Cook for another minute until the raw smell disappears.
5. Stir in the ground coriander, ground cumin, and Kashmiri red chilli powder. Mix well to combine the spices with the onion mixture.
6. Add the tomato puree to the pan and cook for a few minutes until the oil starts to separate from the sauce.
7. Reduce the heat to low and gradually add the heavy cream while stirring continuously. Stir in the honey or sugar and season with salt to taste. Simmer the sauce for about 5 minutes until it thickens slightly.
8. Add the cooked chicken to the sauce and simmer for another 5 minutes, allowing the flavours to meld together. If the sauce is too thick, you can add a little water or more cream to achieve the desired consistency.
9. Garnish the butter chicken with fresh coriander leaves.

Serve the butter chicken hot with naan bread, rice, or roti.

Chettinad Chicken

Chettinad chicken is a flavourful and aromatic dish from the Chettinad region of Tamil Nadu, South India. It is known for its robust flavours, thanks to the blend of spices and the use of freshly ground masala.

For the Marinade

- 500 grams chicken, cut into pieces
- 2 tablespoons yogurt
- 1 tablespoon ginger-garlic paste
- 1 teaspoon red chilli powder
- 1/2 teaspoon turmeric powder
- Salt to taste

For the Chettinad Masala

- 1 tablespoon coriander seeds
- 1 teaspoon cumin seeds
- 1 teaspoon fennel seeds
- 1/2 teaspoon peppercorns
- 4-5 dried red chillies
- 4-5 cloves
- 2-inch cinnamon stick
- 2-3 green cardamom pods
- 2-3 black cardamom pods
- 2-3 curry leaves

For the Chettinad Chicken

- 2 tablespoons oil
- 1 onion, finely chopped
- 2 tomatoes, finely chopped
- 1 tablespoon ginger-garlic paste
- 1 sprig curry leaves
- 1/2 cup coconut milk

- Salt to taste
- Fresh coriander leaves, for garnish

Instructions

1. In a bowl, combine all the marinade ingredients - yogurt, ginger-garlic paste, red chilli powder, turmeric powder, and salt. Mix well. Add the chicken pieces to the marinade, ensuring they are coated evenly. Cover the bowl and let the chicken marinate for at least 1 hour, or overnight in the refrigerator for better flavours.
2. In a dry pan, roast the coriander seeds, cumin seeds, fennel seeds, peppercorns, dried red chillies, cloves, cinnamon stick, green cardamom pods, black cardamom pods, and curry leaves until fragrant. Allow the spices to cool, then grind them to a fine powder using a spice grinder or mortar and pestle.
3. Heat oil in a large pan or kadai over medium heat. Add the chopped onions and sauté until they turn golden brown.
4. Add the ginger-garlic paste and curry leaves to the pan. Cook for a minute until the raw smell disappears.
5. Add the chopped tomatoes to the pan and cook until they become soft and mushy.
6. Stir in the ground Chettinad masala and cook for a couple of minutes to release the flavours.
7. Add the marinated chicken to the pan and mix well, ensuring the chicken is coated with the masala.
8. Cook the chicken on medium heat until it is browned and the oil starts to separate from the masala.
9. Pour in the coconut milk and mix well. Reduce the heat to low, cover the pan, and let the chicken simmer for about 20-25 minutes, or until it is cooked through and tender. Stir occasionally to prevent sticking.
10. Check the seasoning and adjust salt if needed.
11. Garnish the Chettinad chicken with fresh coriander leaves.

South Indian Fish Curry

Also known as Meen Kuzhambu. This flavourful and tangy curry is made with a variety of spices and tamarind for a delightful balance of flavours. Adjust the spice levels and ingredients according to your taste preferences.

Ingredients

- 500g fish fillets (such as tilapia, cod, or snapper), cut into pieces
- 2 tablespoons vegetable oil
- 1 teaspoon mustard seeds
- 1 teaspoon fenugreek seeds
- 1 onion, finely chopped
- 3 cloves of garlic, minced
- 1-inch piece of ginger, grated
- 2 green chillies, slit lengthwise
- 1 sprig of curry leaves
- 2 tomatoes, finely chopped
- 1 teaspoon turmeric powder
- 2 teaspoons red chilli powder (adjust according to spice preference)
- 2 tablespoons tamarind paste (mixed with 1/2 cup water)
- Salt to taste
- Fresh coriander leaves, chopped (for garnish)

Spice Paste

- 2 teaspoons coriander seeds
- 1 teaspoon cumin seeds
- 1/2 teaspoon fenugreek seeds
- 5-6 dried red chillies
- 1/2 cup grated coconut

Instructions

1. In a small pan, dry roast the coriander seeds, cumin seeds, fenugreek seeds, and dried red chillies over low heat until fragrant.

Transfer to a blender or spice grinder and grind into a fine powder. Add the grated coconut to the blender and grind again until you have a smooth paste. Set aside.

2. In a large pan or kadai, heat the vegetable oil over medium heat. Add the mustard seeds and fenugreek seeds. Let them splutter.
3. Add the chopped onions, minced garlic, grated ginger, slit green chillies, and curry leaves to the pan. Sauté until the onions turn golden brown.
4. Stir in the chopped tomatoes and cook until they soften and release their juices.
5. Add the ground spice paste, turmeric powder, and red chilli powder to the pan. Mix well and cook for a couple of minutes to toast the spices.
6. Pour in the tamarind-water mixture, stirring to combine. Bring the curry to a gentle simmer and let it cook for about 10-15 minutes to allow the flavours to meld together.
7. Season with salt to taste. Carefully add the fish fillets to the curry, ensuring they are immersed in the sauce. Simmer for another 5-7 minutes or until the fish is cooked through and flakes easily with a fork.
8. Garnish with freshly chopped coriander leaves.
9. Serve hot with steamed rice or dosa, allowing the fish curry to mingle with the rice or soak up the dosa.

Prawn Masala

This aromatic and rich curry combines succulent prawns with a blend of spices and coconut milk for a truly satisfying dish. Customize the spice levels and ingredients to suit your taste preferences.

Ingredients

- 500g prawns, peeled and deveined
- 2 tablespoons vegetable oil
- 1 onion, finely chopped
- 3 cloves of garlic, minced
- 1-inch piece of ginger, grated
- 2 green chillies, slit lengthwise
- 1 teaspoon mustard seeds
- 1 teaspoon cumin seeds
- 1 teaspoon turmeric powder
- 2 teaspoons red chilli powder (adjust according to spice preference)
- 1 teaspoon ground coriander
- 1 teaspoon ground cumin
- 1 teaspoon garam masala
- 1 cup coconut milk
- 1 cup tomato puree
- Salt to taste
- Fresh coriander leaves, chopped (for garnish)
- Fresh lemon wedges (for serving)

Instructions

1. In a large pan, heat the vegetable oil over medium heat. Add the mustard seeds and cumin seeds. Let them splutter.
2. Add the chopped onions, minced garlic, grated ginger, and slit green chillies to the pan. Sauté until the onions turn golden brown.
3. Stir in the turmeric powder, red chilli powder, ground coriander, ground cumin, and garam masala. Mix well and cook for a couple of minutes to toast the spices.

4. Add the tomato puree to the pan and cook for about 5 minutes, stirring occasionally.
5. Reduce the heat to low and pour in the coconut milk. Stir well to combine and bring the curry to a gentle simmer.
6. Add the prawns to the curry and cook for about 5-7 minutes or until the prawns are cooked through and pink in colour. Be careful not to overcook them, as they can become tough.
7. Season with salt to taste.
8. Garnish with freshly chopped coriander leaves.
9. Serve hot with steamed rice or naan bread. Squeeze fresh lemon juice over the curry for a tangy kick, if desired.

Malai Kofta

Malai Kofta is a popular vegetarian dish in Indian cuisine, consisting of fried potato and paneer (Indian cottage cheese) dumplings served in a rich and creamy tomato-based gravy.

For the koftas (dumplings)

- 2 medium-sized potatoes, boiled and mashed
- 200 grams paneer, grated or crumbled
- 2 tablespoons corn flour or all-purpose flour
- 1 teaspoon ginger paste
- 1 teaspoon garlic paste
- 1 teaspoon garam masala
- 1/2 teaspoon red chilli powder
- Salt to taste
- Oil for deep frying

For the gravy

- 2 tablespoons ghee or vegetable oil
- 1 large onion, finely chopped
- 2 tomatoes, pureed
- 1 teaspoon ginger paste
- 1 teaspoon garlic paste
- 1 teaspoon red chilli powder
- 1 teaspoon turmeric powder
- 1 teaspoon ground coriander
- 1 teaspoon ground cumin
- 1/2 teaspoon garam masala
- 1/2 cup heavy cream or cashew cream
- Salt to taste
- Fresh coriander leaves for garnish

Instructions

1. In a mixing bowl, combine the mashed potatoes, grated paneer, corn flour or all-purpose flour, ginger paste, garlic paste, garam masala, red chilli powder, and salt. Mix well to form a smooth dough-like mixture.
2. Divide the mixture into small portions and shape them into round or oval dumplings (koftas).
3. Heat oil in a deep pan or kadai over medium heat. Once the oil is hot, carefully add the koftas and fry them until golden brown and crisp. Remove them from the oil and set aside on a kitchen towel to drain excess oil.
4. In a separate pan, heat ghee or oil over medium heat. Add the chopped onions and sauté until golden brown.
5. Add ginger paste and garlic paste to the pan and cook for a minute until the raw smell disappears.
6. Add the tomato puree to the pan and cook until the oil separates from the masala.
7. Add red chilli powder, turmeric powder, ground coriander, ground cumin, garam masala, and salt. Mix well and cook for a few minutes.
8. Reduce the heat to low and add the heavy cream or cashew cream to the pan. Stir well to combine the cream with the masala.
9. Simmer the gravy for a few minutes until it thickens slightly. If needed, you can add some water to adjust the consistency.
10. Just before serving, gently add the fried koftas to the gravy and simmer for a few minutes to allow them to soak up the flavours.
11. Garnish with fresh coriander leaves.
12. Serve the hot and creamy Malai Kofta with naan bread, roti, or rice.

Rogan Josh

Rogan Josh is a classic Kashmiri dish known for its rich and aromatic flavours. It traditionally consists of tender pieces of meat cooked in a thick, flavourful sauce.

Ingredients

- 500 grams boneless (or on the bone) lamb, cut into bite-sized pieces
- 3 tablespoons vegetable oil
- 2 medium onions, finely chopped
- 2 teaspoons ginger paste
- 2 teaspoons garlic paste
- 2 teaspoons ground cumin
- 2 teaspoons ground coriander
- 1 teaspoon turmeric powder
- 1 teaspoon Kashmiri red chilli powder (adjust according to spice preference)
- 1 teaspoon paprika (for colour)
- 1/2 teaspoon ground cardamom
- 1/2 teaspoon ground cinnamon
- 1/4 teaspoon ground cloves
- 1 cup plain yogurt, whisked
- 1 cup tomato puree
- 1 cup water (adjust as needed)
- Salt to taste
- Fresh coriander leaves for garnish

Instructions

1. Heat vegetable oil in a deep pan or Dutch oven over medium heat. Add the chopped onions and sauté until golden brown.
2. Add ginger paste and garlic paste to the pan and cook for a minute until the raw smell disappears.
3. Add ground cumin, ground coriander, turmeric powder, Kashmiri red chilli powder, paprika, ground cardamom, ground cinnamon,

and ground cloves. Mix well and cook for a few minutes to toast the spices.

4. Reduce the heat to low and add the whisked yogurt to the pan. Stir well to combine the yogurt with the spices. Cook for a few minutes until the oil starts to separate from the masala.

5. Add the tomato puree to the pan and cook until the oil separates from the masala.

6. Add the lamb pieces to the pan and mix well to coat them evenly with the spice mixture.

7. Pour in water and season with salt to taste. Stir well, cover the pan, and simmer for about 1.5 to 2 hours, or until the lamb is tender and the flavours are well developed. Stir occasionally and add more water if needed.

8. Once the lamb is cooked through, check for seasoning and adjust if necessary.

9. Garnish with fresh coriander leaves.

10. Serve the hot and aromatic Rogan Josh with steamed rice, naan bread, or roti.

Bread

Chapati

Chapati, also known as roti, is a popular and versatile Indian flatbread that is enjoyed with a variety of curries and dishes. Here's a simple and authentic recipe for making soft and delicious chapatis.

Ingredients

- 2 cups whole wheat flour
- 1 teaspoon salt
- 1 tablespoon vegetable oil
- 3/4 to 1 cup warm water (adjust as needed)

Instructions

1. In a large mixing bowl, combine the whole wheat flour and salt.
2. Make a well in the centre of the flour and add the vegetable oil. Mix the oil into the flour using your fingertips until the mixture becomes crumbly.
3. Gradually add warm water to the flour mixture, a little at a time, and mix with your hand or a wooden spoon. Knead the dough until it comes together and forms a smooth and soft ball. The amount of water needed may vary, so adjust as needed to achieve the right consistency.
4. Once the dough is formed, cover it with a damp cloth or plastic wrap and let it rest for at least 15-20 minutes. This allows the gluten to relax and makes the dough easier to roll.
5. After the resting period, divide the dough into small equal-sized portions, roughly the size of a golf ball.
6. Take one portion of the dough and flatten it with your hands. Dust it with some flour and roll it out into a thin, round disc using a rolling pin. Aim for a diameter of about 6-8 inches.
7. Heat a skillet or tawa over medium-high heat. Once hot, carefully place the rolled-out chapati onto the skillet.
8. Cook the chapati for about 30 seconds to a minute, or until you start seeing bubbles forming on the surface. Flip it over and cook the

other side for another 30 seconds to a minute. You may need to gently press down on the chapati with a spatula to help it puff up.

9. Once both sides are cooked and lightly browned, remove the chapati from the skillet and place it in a clean kitchen towel or a covered container to keep it soft and warm. Repeat the process with the remaining portions of dough.

10. Serve the freshly cooked chapatis with your favourite curries, vegetables, or dips.

Enjoy the soft and delicious chapatis as a staple accompaniment to your Indian meals. They are perfect for scooping up curries or as a wrap for various fillings. Experiment with different toppings and fillings to create your own variations.

Naan

While traditionally naan bread is cooked in a tandoor oven, you can still achieve delicious results by making naan in a conventional oven. Here's a recipe for making naan bread in a conventional oven.

Ingredients

- 2 cups all-purpose flour
- 1 teaspoon instant yeast
- 1 teaspoon sugar
- 1/2 teaspoon salt
- 1/4 teaspoon baking powder
- 2 tablespoons plain yogurt
- 2 tablespoons vegetable oil
- 1/2 cup warm milk
- Butter or ghee, melted (for brushing)
- Fresh coriander leaves (optional, for garnish)

Instructions

1. In a small bowl, combine the warm milk, sugar, and instant yeast. Stir well and let it sit for about 5 minutes until the yeast is activated and becomes frothy.
2. In a large mixing bowl, combine the all-purpose flour, salt, and baking powder.
3. Make a well in the centre of the flour mixture and add the activated yeast mixture, yogurt, and vegetable oil.
4. Gradually mix the wet ingredients into the flour until a dough forms. You may need to add a little more warm milk or water if the dough is too dry or flour if it's too sticky.
5. Transfer the dough onto a lightly floured surface and knead it for about 5-7 minutes until it becomes smooth and elastic.
6. Place the dough in a greased bowl, cover it with a clean kitchen towel or plastic wrap, and let it rise in a warm place for about 1 to 1.5 hours until it doubles in size.

7. Preheat your conventional oven to the highest temperature setting (usually around 500°F or 260°C) and place a baking stone or a baking sheet on the middle rack to heat up.
8. Once the dough has risen, divide it into small equal-sized portions (around 8-10) and roll each portion into a teardrop or oval shape, about 1/4-inch thick.
9. Carefully place the rolled-out naan onto the preheated baking stone or baking sheet in the oven.
10. Bake the naan for about 2-3 minutes until it puffs up and starts to develop golden brown spots. You can also turn on the broiler for the last 30 seconds to 1 minute to get a nice char on top, but be careful not to burn them.
11. Remove the naan from the oven and immediately brush it with melted butter or ghee. Sprinkle fresh coriander leaves over the top if desired.
12. Serve the naan bread warm and enjoy it with your favourite curries or dips.

Making naan bread in a conventional oven may not replicate the exact texture and flavour of tandoor-cooked naan, but it will still result in a tasty and soft bread that complements your Indian meals perfectly.

Puri

Puri is a popular Indian fried bread that is soft, fluffy, and perfect to accompany various dishes like curries or chutneys.

Ingredients

- 2 cups whole wheat flour
- 1/2 teaspoon salt
- 1 tablespoon vegetable oil
- Warm water (as needed)
- Vegetable oil (for frying)

Instructions

1. In a large mixing bowl, combine the whole wheat flour and salt. Mix well.
2. Make a well in the centre of the flour mixture and add the vegetable oil.
3. Gradually add warm water, a little at a time, and knead the dough until it comes together. The dough should be soft and pliable but not too sticky. Adjust the water as needed.
4. Once the dough is formed, continue kneading it for about 5-7 minutes until it becomes smooth and elastic.
5. Cover the dough with a damp cloth or plastic wrap and let it rest for about 15-20 minutes. This helps to relax the gluten and make the puris soft.
6. After the resting period, divide the dough into small equal-sized balls, approximately the size of a golf ball.
7. Heat vegetable oil in a deep frying pan or kadai over medium-high heat.
8. Take a dough ball and roll it into a small disc using a rolling pin. The disc should be about 4-5 inches in diameter and of even thickness.
9. Carefully slide the rolled puri into the hot oil and gently press it with a slotted spoon. This helps the puri to puff up.

10. Fry the puri for about 30-40 seconds on one side until it turns golden brown. Then, flip it over and fry the other side for another 30-40 seconds.
11. Once the puri is evenly fried and puffed up, remove it from the oil using a slotted spoon and transfer it to a plate lined with paper towels to absorb any excess oil.
12. Repeat the process with the remaining dough balls, rolling and frying one puri at a time.
13. Serve the hot and crispy puris immediately with your favourite curry, chutney, or any other accompaniment of your choice.

Enjoy the delightful and fluffy Puris as a delicious side dish or as a snack. They are best enjoyed fresh and warm!

Paratha

Paratha is a delicious and versatile Indian flatbread that is flaky, layered, and perfect to accompany various curries, chutneys, or even enjoyed on its own.

Ingredients

- 2 cups whole wheat flour
- 1/2 teaspoon salt
- 1 tablespoon vegetable oil or ghee
- Water (as needed)
- Extra flour for dusting
- Extra oil or ghee for cooking

Instructions

1. In a large mixing bowl, combine the whole wheat flour and salt. Mix well.
2. Make a well in the centre of the flour mixture and add the vegetable oil or ghee.
3. Gradually add water, a little at a time, and knead the dough until it comes together. The dough should be soft and pliable but not too sticky. Adjust the water as needed.
4. Once the dough is formed, continue kneading it for about 5-7 minutes until it becomes smooth and elastic.
5. Cover the dough with a damp cloth or plastic wrap and let it rest for about 15-20 minutes. This helps to relax the gluten and make the parathas soft.
6. After the resting period, divide the dough into small equal-sized balls, approximately the size of a golf ball.
7. Take one dough ball and flatten it with your hands. Dust it with some flour and roll it out into a thin, round disc using a rolling pin. The disc should be approximately 6-8 inches in diameter.
8. Brush the rolled disc with a little oil or ghee, spreading it evenly.
9. Starting from one edge, make pleats on the disc by folding it inwards, creating a layered fan-like shape.

10. Once the pleats are formed, roll the layered disc into a spiral or coil shape.
11. Flatten the spiral gently with your palm and dust it with flour.
12. Roll out the flattened spiral again into a round paratha, making sure it is of even thickness and approximately 6-8 inches in diameter.
13. Heat a tawa or griddle over medium-high heat. Place the rolled paratha on the hot tawa and cook for about 30-40 seconds until you see bubbles forming on the surface.
14. Flip the paratha and apply a little oil or ghee on the cooked side. Cook for another 30-40 seconds.
15. Flip it again and apply oil or ghee on the second side as well. Cook for a few more seconds until both sides are golden brown and cooked through.
16. Remove the cooked paratha from the tawa and transfer it to a plate. Keep it covered with a clean cloth or foil to keep it warm.
17. Repeat the process with the remaining dough balls, rolling, layering, and cooking one paratha at a time.
18. Serve the hot and flaky parathas immediately with your favourite curry, chutney, or any other accompaniment of your choice.

Enjoy the delicious and flaky Parathas as a delightful addition to your meals. They are best enjoyed fresh and warm!

Aloo Paratha

Aloo Paratha is a delicious and popular Indian stuffed bread made with a spiced potato filling. It is a perfect combination of soft and flaky bread with a flavourful potato filling.

For the dough

- 2 cups whole wheat flour
- 1 teaspoon salt
- Water, as needed for kneading
- 2 tablespoons ghee or vegetable oil

For the potato filling

- 3 medium-sized potatoes, boiled, peeled, and mashed
- 1 small onion, finely chopped
- 2 green chillies, finely chopped
- 1 teaspoon grated ginger
- 1/2 teaspoon cumin seeds
- 1/2 teaspoon red chilli powder (adjust according to spice preference)
- 1/2 teaspoon garam masala powder
- 1/2 teaspoon turmeric powder
- Salt to taste
- Fresh coriander leaves, finely chopped

Instructions

1. In a mixing bowl, combine the whole wheat flour and salt. Gradually add water and knead to form a smooth and soft dough. Drizzle a little ghee or oil over the dough, cover it, and let it rest for about 30 minutes.
2. In a separate bowl, combine the mashed potatoes, chopped onions, green chillies, grated ginger, cumin seeds, red chilli powder, garam masala powder, turmeric powder, salt, and chopped fresh coriander leaves. Mix well to combine all the ingredients.

3. Divide the dough into equal-sized balls. Take one dough ball and roll it into a small circle, approximately 4-5 inches in diameter.
4. Place a portion of the potato filling in the centre of the rolled dough circle. Bring the edges of the dough together to seal the filling inside, forming a stuffed ball.
5. Gently flatten the stuffed ball and dust it with flour. Roll it out into a round paratha, about 6-7 inches in diameter. Be careful not to apply too much pressure while rolling, as it may break and release the filling.
6. Heat a tawa or griddle over medium heat. Place the rolled paratha on the hot tawa and cook for a minute or until you see bubbles forming on the surface.
7. Flip the paratha and spread a little ghee or oil on the surface. Cook for another minute until golden brown spots appear.
8. Flip again and apply ghee or oil on the other side. Press the edges gently with a spatula to ensure even cooking.
9. Cook the paratha on both sides until it is golden brown and cooked through.
10. Remove the paratha from the tawa and repeat the process with the remaining dough and filling.
11. Serve the hot and freshly cooked Aloo Parathas with yogurt, pickle, or any chutney of your choice.

Aloo Paratha is a versatile dish that can be enjoyed for breakfast, lunch, or dinner. The combination of the soft paratha and flavourful potato filling is simply irresistible.

Rice

Plain Basmati Rice

Basmati rice is a fragrant and long-grain rice variety that is popular for its distinct aroma and fluffy texture.

Ingredients

- 1 cup basmati rice
- 1 ¾ cups water
- 1 tablespoon ghee or vegetable oil
- Salt to taste

Instructions

1. Rinse the basmati rice under cold water until the water runs clear. This helps remove excess starch and ensures the rice cooks evenly.
2. Soak the rice in water for 30 minutes. This step helps the rice grains expand and results in a fluffier texture.
3. After soaking, drain the rice and set it aside.
4. In a medium-sized saucepan, heat the ghee or vegetable oil over medium heat.
5. Add the drained rice to the pan and sauté for a couple of minutes, stirring gently to coat each grain with the ghee or oil. This step helps prevent the rice from sticking together.
6. Add the water to the pan and season with salt. Stir gently to combine.
7. Bring the water to a boil over high heat.
8. Once the water comes to a boil, reduce the heat to low and cover the saucepan with a tight-fitting lid.
9. Let the rice simmer undisturbed for about 15-20 minutes or until all the water has been absorbed and the rice is tender.
10. Once the rice is cooked, remove the saucepan from heat and let it sit, covered, for another 5 minutes. This allows the steam to distribute evenly and ensures fluffy rice grains.
11. Fluff the rice gently with a fork to separate the grains.

Your perfect basmati rice is ready to be served as a delicious side dish to accompany various curries, stir-fries, or other main courses. Enjoy the fragrant and fluffy basmati rice!

Pilau Rice

One of the most flavourful and aromatic rice dishes is Pilau, also known as Pulao or Pilaf. This dish is made by cooking rice with a blend of spices.

Ingredients

- 1 ½ cups basmati rice
- 2 tablespoons ghee or vegetable oil
- 1 onion, thinly sliced
- 2 cloves of garlic, minced
- 1-inch piece of ginger, grated
- 1 cinnamon stick
- 4 green cardamom pods
- 4 whole cloves
- 1 bay leaf
- 1 teaspoon cumin seeds
- 1 teaspoon turmeric powder
- 1 teaspoon ground coriander
- 1 teaspoon garam masala
- 2 cups water or vegetable broth
- Salt to taste
- Chopped fresh coriander leaves (for garnish)

Optional Additions

- ½ cup mixed vegetables (such as carrots, peas, and bell peppers), diced
- ½ cup cooked meat (such as chicken, beef, or lamb), diced

Instructions

1. Rinse the basmati rice under cold water until the water runs clear. This helps remove excess starch and ensures the rice cooks evenly.
2. Soak the rice in water for 30 minutes. This step helps the rice grains expand and results in a fluffier texture.

3. After soaking, drain the rice and set it aside.
4. In a large saucepan or Dutch oven, heat the ghee or vegetable oil over medium heat.
5. Add the sliced onions to the pan and sauté until they turn golden brown and caramelized.
6. Add the minced garlic, grated ginger, cinnamon stick, cardamom pods, cloves, bay leaf, and cumin seeds to the pan. Sauté for a couple of minutes until the spices become fragrant.
7. If using vegetables and/or meat, add them to the pan and sauté for a few minutes until they are slightly cooked.
8. Stir in the turmeric powder, ground coriander, and garam masala. Mix well to coat the onions and spices.
9. Add the drained rice to the pan and stir gently to combine with the spices and vegetables/meat.
10. Pour in the water or vegetable broth, along with salt to taste. Stir gently to ensure even distribution of flavours.
11. Bring the mixture to a boil over high heat, then reduce the heat to low and cover the pan with a tight-fitting lid.
12. Let the rice simmer undisturbed for about 15-20 minutes or until all the liquid has been absorbed and the rice is tender.
13. Once the rice is cooked, remove the pan from heat and let it sit, covered, for another 5 minutes. This allows the steam to distribute evenly and ensures fluffy rice grains.
14. Fluff the rice gently with a fork to separate the grains.
15. Garnish with freshly chopped coriander leaves.

Veg Pilau

Veg Pilau, also known as Vegetable Pulao, is a delightful and aromatic rice dish that combines fragrant basmati rice with an assortment of vegetables and flavourful spices.

Ingredients

- 2 cups basmati rice
- 4 cups water
- 2 tablespoons ghee or vegetable oil
- 1 onion, thinly sliced
- 2 cloves of garlic, minced
- 1-inch piece of ginger, grated
- 1 green chilli, slit lengthwise
- 1 cinnamon stick
- 4 green cardamom pods
- 4 whole cloves
- 1 bay leaf
- 1 teaspoon cumin seeds
- 1 teaspoon turmeric powder
- 1 teaspoon red chilli powder (adjust according to spice preference)
- 1 teaspoon ground coriander
- 1 teaspoon garam masala
- 1 cup mixed vegetables (such as carrots, peas, bell peppers, and cauliflower), diced
- Salt to taste
- Fresh coriander leaves, chopped (for garnish)
- Fried onions (for garnish)

Instructions

1. Rinse the basmati rice under cold water until the water runs clear. This helps remove excess starch and ensures the rice cooks evenly.
2. Soak the rice in water for 30 minutes. This step helps the rice grains expand and results in a fluffier texture.
3. After soaking, drain the rice and set it aside.

4. In a large saucepan or Dutch oven, heat the ghee or vegetable oil over medium heat.
5. Add the sliced onions to the pan and sauté until they turn golden brown and caramelized.
6. Add the minced garlic, grated ginger, green chilli, cinnamon stick, cardamom pods, cloves, bay leaf, and cumin seeds to the pan. Sauté for a couple of minutes until the spices become fragrant.
7. Add the diced vegetables to the pan and sauté for a few minutes until they are slightly cooked.
8. Stir in the turmeric powder, red chilli powder, ground coriander, and garam masala. Mix well to coat the vegetables with the spices.
9. Add the soaked and drained rice to the pan. Gently mix the rice with the vegetables and spices, taking care not to break the rice grains.
10. Pour in the water. Stir gently to ensure all the ingredients are well combined.
11. Bring the mixture to a boil over high heat. Once it starts boiling, reduce the heat to low and cover the pan with a tight-fitting lid.
12. Let the pilau simmer for about 15-20 minutes or until all the liquid has been absorbed and the rice is cooked through. Be careful not to overcook the rice.
13. Once the rice is cooked, remove the pan from heat and let it sit, covered, for another 5 minutes. This allows the flavours to meld together and ensures fluffy rice grains.
14. Fluff the rice gently with a fork to separate the grains.
15. Garnish with freshly chopped coriander leaves and fried onions.

Jeera Rice

Ingredients

- 1 cup basmati rice
- 2 cups water
- 2 tablespoons ghee or vegetable oil
- 1 teaspoon cumin seeds (jeera)
- 1 small onion, finely chopped
- 2-3 green chilies, slit lengthwise
- 1-inch piece of ginger, grated
- Salt to taste
- Fresh coriander leaves, chopped (for garnish)

Instructions

1. Wash the basmati rice thoroughly under running water until the water runs clear. Soak for 30 minutes, then drain and set aside.
2. In a saucepan or a pot, heat the ghee or vegetable oil over medium heat.
3. Add the cumin seeds to the hot oil and let them sizzle and release their aroma for a few seconds.
4. Add the chopped onion, green chilies, and grated ginger to the pan. Sauté until the onions turn translucent and lightly golden.
5. Add the drained basmati rice to the pan and stir well to coat the rice with the onion mixture and oil.
6. Pour in the water and season with salt according to your taste. Stir gently to combine.
7. Increase the heat to high and bring the water to a boil. Once it starts boiling, reduce the heat to low, cover the pan with a tight-fitting lid, and simmer for about 15-20 minutes or until the rice is cooked and all the water has been absorbed.
8. Once the rice is cooked, turn off the heat and let it sit, covered, for 5-10 minutes. This will help the rice grains fluff up.
9. After resting, remove the lid and fluff the rice gently with a fork to separate the grains.

Biryani

Vegetable Biryani

Vegetable Biryani is a popular and flavourful rice dish that combines aromatic spices, fragrant basmati rice, and an assortment of vegetables.

Ingredients

- 2 cups basmati rice
- 4 cups water
- 2 tablespoons ghee or vegetable oil
- 1 onion, thinly sliced
- 2 cloves of garlic, minced
- 1-inch piece of ginger, grated
- 1 green chilli, slit lengthwise
- 1 cinnamon stick
- 4 green cardamom pods
- 4 whole cloves
- 1 bay leaf
- 1 teaspoon cumin seeds
- 1 teaspoon turmeric powder
- 1 teaspoon red chilli powder (adjust according to spice preference)
- 1 teaspoon ground coriander
- 1 teaspoon garam masala
- 1 cup mixed vegetables (such as carrots, peas, bell peppers, and cauliflower), diced
- 1 cup plain yogurt
- Salt to taste
- Fresh coriander leaves, chopped (for garnish)
- Fried onions (for garnish)

Instructions

1. Rinse the basmati rice under cold water until the water runs clear. This helps remove excess starch and ensures the rice cooks evenly.
2. Soak the rice in water for 30 minutes. This step helps the rice grains expand and results in a fluffier texture.

3. After soaking, drain the rice and set it aside.
4. In a large saucepan or Dutch oven, heat the ghee or vegetable oil over medium heat.
5. Add the sliced onions to the pan and sauté until they turn golden brown and caramelized.
6. Add the minced garlic, grated ginger, green chilli, cinnamon stick, cardamom pods, cloves, bay leaf, and cumin seeds to the pan. Sauté for a couple of minutes until the spices become fragrant.
7. Add the diced vegetables to the pan and sauté for a few minutes until they are slightly cooked.
8. Stir in the turmeric powder, red chilli powder, ground coriander, and garam masala. Mix well to coat the vegetables with the spices.
9. Add the soaked and drained rice to the pan. Gently mix the rice with the vegetables and spices, taking care not to break the rice grains.
10. Pour in the water and plain yogurt. Stir gently to ensure all the ingredients are well combined.
11. Bring the mixture to a boil over high heat. Once it starts boiling, reduce the heat to low and cover the pan with a tight-fitting lid.
12. Let the biryani simmer for about 15-20 minutes or until all the liquid has been absorbed and the rice is cooked through. Be careful not to overcook the rice.
13. Once the rice is cooked, remove the pan from heat and let it sit, covered, for another 5 minutes. This allows the flavours to meld together and ensures fluffy rice grains.
14. Fluff the rice gently with a fork to separate the grains.
15. Garnish with freshly chopped coriander leaves and fried onions.

Lamb Biryani

Lamb Biryani is a rich and aromatic rice dish that combines succulent pieces of lamb with fragrant basmati rice and a blend of spices.

For the Rice

- 2 cups basmati rice
- 4 cups water
- 1 teaspoon salt

For the Lamb

- 500g lamb, cut into pieces
- 2 tablespoons vegetable oil
- 1 large onion, thinly sliced
- 2 cloves of garlic, minced
- 1-inch piece of ginger, grated
- 2 green chillies, slit lengthwise
- 1 cinnamon stick
- 4 green cardamom pods
- 4 whole cloves
- 1 bay leaf
- 1 teaspoon cumin seeds
- 1 teaspoon coriander powder
- 1 teaspoon turmeric powder
- 1 teaspoon red chilli powder (adjust according to spice preference)
- 1 teaspoon garam masala
- 1 cup plain yogurt
- Salt to taste
- Fresh coriander leaves, chopped (for garnish)
- Fried onions (for garnish)
- Saffron strands (optional, soaked in 2 tablespoons of warm milk)

Instructions

1. Rinse the basmati rice under cold water until the water runs clear. This helps remove excess starch and ensures the rice cooks evenly.
2. Soak the rice in water for 30 minutes. This step helps the rice grains expand and results in a fluffier texture.
3. After soaking, drain the rice and set it aside.
4. In a large pot, bring 4 cups of water to a boil. Add the drained rice and 1 teaspoon of salt. Cook the rice until it is 70-80% cooked (al dente). Drain and set aside.
5. In a separate pan, heat the vegetable oil over medium heat. Add the sliced onions and sauté until they turn golden brown and caramelized.
6. Add the minced garlic, grated ginger, green chillies, cinnamon stick, cardamom pods, cloves, bay leaf, and cumin seeds to the pan. Sauté for a couple of minutes until the spices become fragrant.
7. Add the lamb pieces to the pan and cook until they are browned on all sides.
8. Stir in the coriander powder, turmeric powder, red chilli powder, and garam masala. Mix well to coat the lamb with the spices.
9. Add the plain yogurt to the pan and mix well to combine with the spices and lamb. Cook for a few minutes until the yogurt is well incorporated.
10. Season with salt to taste. Add a splash of water if needed to create a thick gravy. Cover the pan and let the lamb simmer for about 45-60 minutes or until it is tender and cooked through.
11. Preheat your oven to 180°C (350°F).
12. In a large oven-safe dish, layer half of the cooked rice at the bottom. Top it with the cooked lamb and its gravy, spreading it evenly.
13. Layer the remaining rice on top of the lamb. If desired, drizzle the saffron-infused milk. .
14. Cover the dish tightly with aluminium foil or a lid. Place it in the preheated oven and bake for 20-25 minutes to allow the flavours to meld together and the rice to fully cook.
15. Remove the dish from the oven. Garnish with freshly chopped coriander leaves and fried onions.

Bombay Biryani

Bombay biryani, also known as Mumbai biryani, is a flavourful and aromatic rice dish that originates from the city of Mumbai in India. It is a delightful blend of fragrant basmati rice, tender meat (typically chicken or mutton), and a medley of spices.

Ingredients

For the marinade

- 500 grams chicken or mutton, cut into pieces
- 1 cup plain yogurt
- 2 tablespoons ginger-garlic paste
- 1 teaspoon turmeric powder
- 1 teaspoon red chilli powder
- 1 teaspoon garam masala powder
- Salt to taste

For the rice

- 2 cups basmati rice, soaked in water for 30 minutes and drained
- 4 cups water
- 2-3 green cardamom pods
- 1 cinnamon stick
- 2-3 cloves
- Salt to taste

For the biryani

- 3 tablespoons ghee or vegetable oil
- 2 onions, thinly sliced
- 2 tomatoes, chopped
- 2 green chillies, slit lengthwise
- 1 tablespoon ginger-garlic paste
- 1 teaspoon cumin seeds
- 1 teaspoon coriander powder

- 1 teaspoon red chilli powder
- 1/2 teaspoon turmeric powder
- 1/2 teaspoon garam masala powder
- Fresh coriander leaves for garnish
- Fried onions for garnish (optional)
- Lemon wedges for serving

Instructions

1. In a mixing bowl, combine the chicken or mutton pieces with yogurt, ginger-garlic paste, turmeric powder, red chilli powder, garam masala powder, and salt. Mix well to coat the meat. Let it marinate for at least 30 minutes, or refrigerate for a few hours to enhance the flavours.
2. In a large pot, bring 4 cups of water to a boil. Add the soaked and drained basmati rice, along with green cardamom pods, cinnamon stick, cloves, and salt. Cook the rice until it is 70-80% cooked (parboiled). Drain the rice and set aside.
3. Heat ghee or oil in a large, heavy-bottomed pan or pot over medium heat. Add the thinly sliced onions and sauté until they turn golden brown and crispy. Remove a portion of the fried onions and set them aside for garnishing.
4. To the remaining fried onions in the pan, add the chopped tomatoes, green chillies, and ginger-garlic paste. Cook until the tomatoes are soft and well-cooked.
5. Add cumin seeds, coriander powder, red chilli powder, turmeric powder, and garam masala powder to the pan. Stir well to combine the spices with the onion and tomato mixture.
6. Add the marinated chicken or mutton to the pan and cook on medium heat until the meat is partially cooked and the spices are well-incorporated, about 8-10 minutes.
7. Layer the parboiled rice over the meat mixture in the pan. Sprinkle some fresh coriander leaves and fried onions (if using) over the rice.
8. Cover the pan with a tight-fitting lid and cook on low heat for about 20-25 minutes, or until the rice is fully cooked and the flavours have melded together. You can also place a tawa (flat pan) underneath the biryani pot to prevent the bottom from burning.

9. Once cooked, remove the pan from heat and let it rest, covered, for 10 minutes to allow the flavours to intensify.
10. Gently fluff

Hydrabadi Biryani

Hyderabadi biryani is a rich and aromatic rice dish from the city of Hyderabad in India. It is known for its flavourful spices and tender meat or vegetables.

For the rice

- 2 cups basmati rice
- 4 cups water
- 2-3 green cardamom pods
- 1 cinnamon stick
- 2-3 cloves
- Salt to taste

For the biryani

- 500 grams chicken (cut into pieces) or vegetables of your choice
- 1 cup plain yogurt
- 2 tablespoons ginger-garlic paste
- 2 medium-sized onions, thinly sliced
- 1/2 cup chopped fresh mint leaves
- 1/2 cup chopped fresh coriander leaves
- 2-3 green chillies, slit lengthwise
- 1 teaspoon turmeric powder
- 1 teaspoon red chilli powder (adjust according to spice preference)
- 1 teaspoon biryani masala powder (optional)
- 1/2 teaspoon saffron strands, soaked in 2 tablespoons warm milk
- 1/4 cup ghee (clarified butter) or vegetable oil
- Salt to taste

For the garnish

- Fried onions (from the sliced onions)
- Chopped fresh mint leaves
- Chopped fresh coriander leaves
- Fried cashews and raisins (optional)

Instructions

1. Rinse the basmati rice under running water until the water runs clear. Soak the rice in water for 30 minutes, then drain and set aside.
2. In a large pot, bring 4 cups of water to a boil. Add the soaked and drained rice, along with green cardamom pods, cinnamon stick, cloves, and salt. Cook the rice until it is 70-80% cooked (parboiled). Drain the rice and set aside.
3. In a mixing bowl, marinate the chicken or vegetables with yogurt, ginger-garlic paste, turmeric powder, red chilli powder, biryani masala powder (if using), and salt. Let it marinate for at least 30 minutes, or refrigerate for a few hours for the flavours to develop.
4. Heat ghee or oil in a large, heavy-bottomed pan or pot over medium heat. Add the thinly sliced onions and cook until they turn golden brown and crispy. Remove a portion of the fried onions and set them aside for garnishing.
5. To the remaining fried onions in the pan, add the marinated chicken or vegetables. Cook for a few minutes until they are lightly browned.
6. Add chopped mint leaves, chopped coriander leaves, and slit green chillies to the pan. Stir well to combine the flavours.
7. Layer the parboiled rice over the chicken or vegetable mixture in the pan. Drizzle the saffron-soaked milk over the rice.
8. Cover the pan with a tight-fitting lid and cook on low heat for about 20-25 minutes, or until the rice and chicken or vegetables are fully cooked and tender.
9. Once cooked, remove the pan from heat and let it rest, covered, for 10 minutes to allow the flavours to meld.
   Gently fluff the rice with a fork.
   Garnish the Hyderabadi biryani with fried onions, chopped mint leaves, chopped coriander leaves, and fried cashews and raisins (if using).

Prawn Biryani

Prawn Biryani is a delicious and aromatic rice dish that combines succulent prawns with fragrant basmati rice and a blend of spices.

For the Rice

- 2 cups basmati rice
- 4 cups water
- 1 teaspoon salt

For the Prawn Marinade

- 500g prawns, cleaned and deveined
- 2 tablespoons plain yogurt
- 1 teaspoon ginger paste
- 1 teaspoon garlic paste
- 1 teaspoon red chilli powder
- 1/2 teaspoon turmeric powder
- Salt to taste

For the Biryani

- 2 tablespoons ghee or vegetable oil
- 1 onion, thinly sliced
- 2 cloves of garlic, minced
- 1-inch piece of ginger, grated
- 2 green chillies, slit lengthwise
- 1 cinnamon stick
- 4 green cardamom pods
- 4 whole cloves
- 1 bay leaf
- 1 teaspoon cumin seeds
- 1 teaspoon coriander powder
- 1 teaspoon red chilli powder (adjust according to spice preference)
- 1/2 teaspoon turmeric powder
- 1/2 teaspoon garam masala

- 1/4 cup chopped mint leaves
- 1/4 cup chopped coriander leaves
- Salt to taste

Instructions

1. Rinse the basmati rice under cold water until the water runs clear. This helps remove excess starch and ensures the rice cooks evenly.
2. Soak the rice in water for 30 minutes. This step helps the rice grains expand and results in a fluffier texture.
3. After soaking, drain the rice and set it aside.
4. In a bowl, mix together the ingredients for the prawn marinade - plain yogurt, ginger paste, garlic paste, red chilli powder, turmeric powder, and salt. Add the prawns to the marinade and let them sit for 15-20 minutes.
5. In a large pot, bring 4 cups of water to a boil. Add the drained rice and 1 teaspoon of salt. Cook the rice until it is 70-80% cooked (al dente). Drain and set aside.
6. In a separate pan, heat the ghee or vegetable oil over medium heat. Add the sliced onions and sauté until they turn golden brown.
7. Add the minced garlic, grated ginger, green chillies, cinnamon stick, cardamom pods, cloves, bay leaf, and cumin seeds to the pan. Sauté for a couple of minutes until the spices become fragrant.
8. Add the marinated prawns to the pan. Cook for 2-3 minutes until the prawns turn pink and are partially cooked.
9. Stir in the coriander powder, red chilli powder, turmeric powder, and garam masala. Mix well to coat the prawns with the spices.
10. Add the cooked rice to the pan, gently layering it over the prawns. Sprinkle the chopped mint leaves and coriander leaves on top.
11. Cover the pan with a tight-fitting lid and cook on low heat for 15-20 minutes to allow the flavours to meld together and the prawns to fully cook.
12. Remove the pan from heat and let it sit, covered, for another 5 minutes. This allows the flavours to further develop and ensures the rice grains are fully cooked.
13. Gently fluff the biryani with a fork to mix the rice and prawns.
14. Serve the Prawn Biryani hot, garnished with additional mint leaves

Fish Biryani

Ingredients

- 500 grams fish fillets (any firm white fish like cod or tilapia), cut into pieces
- 2 cups basmati rice
- 1 large onion, thinly sliced
- 2 tomatoes, finely chopped
- 2 tablespoons biryani masala powder
- 1 tablespoon ginger-garlic paste
- 1 teaspoon turmeric powder
- 1 teaspoon red chili powder
- 1 teaspoon cumin powder
- 1 teaspoon coriander powder
- 1/2 cup plain yogurt
- 1/4 cup chopped mint leaves
- 1/4 cup chopped coriander leaves
- 4 cups water
- 1/4 cup ghee or vegetable oil
- Salt to taste

For the marinade

- 2 tablespoons lemon juice
- 1 teaspoon turmeric powder
- 1 teaspoon red chili powder
- 1/2 teaspoon salt

For garnish

- Fried onions
- Chopped coriander leaves
- Fried cashew nuts and raisins (optional)

Instructions

1. Wash the basmati rice thoroughly and soak it in water for 30 minutes. Drain and set aside.
2. In a bowl, combine the fish pieces with the marinade ingredients: lemon juice, turmeric powder, red chili powder, and salt. Mix well and let it marinate for 15-20 minutes.
3. Heat ghee or vegetable oil in a large, deep pan or Dutch oven over medium heat. Add the sliced onions and sauté until they turn golden brown and crispy. Remove half of the fried onions and set them aside for garnish.
4. In the same pan with the remaining fried onions, add ginger-garlic paste and sauté for a minute until fragrant.
5. Add the chopped tomatoes and cook until they soften and release their juices.
6. Add the biryani masala powder, turmeric powder, red chili powder, cumin powder, and coriander powder. Mix well and cook for a minute to toast the spices.
7. Add the marinated fish pieces to the pan and gently toss them with the spices. Cook for 2-3 minutes until the fish starts to firm up slightly. Be careful not to overcook the fish.
8. In a separate pot, bring 4 cups of water to a boil. Add the soaked and drained basmati rice to the boiling water. Cook the rice until it is 70-80% cooked. Drain the rice and set it aside.
9. In the same pan with the fish, spread half of the partially cooked rice over the fish layer. Sprinkle half of the chopped mint leaves and coriander leaves on top.
10. Spread the remaining rice over the first layer and top it with the remaining mint leaves, coriander leaves, and fried onions.
11. Cover the pan with a tight-fitting lid and cook on low heat for 15-20 minutes, allowing the flavours to meld and the rice to fully cook.
12. Once done, remove the lid and gently fluff the rice with a fork, being careful not to break the fish pieces.
13. Serve the Fish Biryani hot, garnished with fried onions, chopped coriander leaves, and optionally fried cashew nuts and raisins. Enjoy!

Side Dishes

Tadka Dal

This Tadka Dal recipe offers a delightful combination of lentils, spices, and aromatic tempering. Adjust the spice levels and ingredients according to your taste preferences.

IIngredients

- 1 cup yellow split lentils (toor dal)
- 4 cups water
- 2 tablespoons ghee (clarified butter) or vegetable oil
- 1 teaspoon cumin seeds
- 1 medium onion, finely chopped
- 2 cloves of garlic, minced
- 1-inch piece of ginger, grated
- 2 tomatoes, finely chopped
- 1 teaspoon turmeric powder
- 1 teaspoon red chilli powder (adjust according to spice preference)
- Salt to taste
- Fresh coriander leaves, chopped (for garnish)
- Fresh lemon wedges (for serving)

For Tadka (Tempering)

- 2 tablespoons ghee (clarified butter) or vegetable oil
- 1 teaspoon cumin seeds
- 1 teaspoon mustard seeds
- 1 small dried red chilli (optional)
- A pinch of asafoetida (hing)
- 4-5 curry leaves

Instructions

1. Rinse the yellow split lentils thoroughly and drain. In a large saucepan, combine the lentils and water. Bring to a boil, then reduce the heat to low and simmer, partially covered, for about 30-40

minutes or until the lentils are soft and mushy. Stir occasionally and skim off any foam that forms on the surface.

2. In a separate pan, heat ghee or vegetable oil over medium heat. Add the cumin seeds and let them splutter. Then add the chopped onions and sauté until golden brown.

3. Add the minced garlic and grated ginger to the pan and cook for another minute, stirring constantly.

4. Stir in the chopped tomatoes, turmeric powder, and red chilli powder. Cook for about 5 minutes until the tomatoes have softened and the mixture has thickened.

5. Add the cooked lentils to the tomato-onion mixture, including any remaining water. Mix well and simmer for another 10 minutes to allow the flavours to blend. If the dal seems too thick, you can add some water to achieve the desired consistency.

6. Season with salt to taste and simmer for a few more minutes. Turn off the heat.

7. For the tadka (tempering), heat ghee or vegetable oil in a small pan. Add the cumin seeds, mustard seeds, dried red chilli (if using), asafoetida, and curry leaves. Let them sizzle and release their flavours for a few seconds. Pour this tadka over the cooked dal and mix well.

8. Garnish with freshly chopped coriander leaves.

9. Serve hot with steamed rice or naan bread. Squeeze fresh lemon juice over the dal for a tangy kick, if desired.

Chana Masala

This Chana Masala recipe showcases the earthy flavours of chickpeas combined with a medley of aromatic spices. Customize the spice levels and ingredients to suit your taste preferences.

Ingredients

- 2 cups cooked chickpeas (or 2 cans, drained and rinsed)
- 2 tablespoons vegetable oil
- 1 large onion, finely chopped
- 3 cloves of garlic, minced
- 1-inch piece of ginger, grated
- 2 teaspoons ground cumin
- 2 teaspoons ground coriander
- 1 teaspoon turmeric powder
- 1 teaspoon paprika
- 1 teaspoon garam masala
- 1 teaspoon cumin seeds
- 1 can (400g) diced tomatoes
- 1 cup water or vegetable broth
- Salt to taste
- Fresh coriander leaves, chopped (for garnish)
- Fresh lemon wedges (for serving)

Instructions

1. Heat the vegetable oil in a large pan over medium heat. Add the cumin seeds and sauté until they begin to splutter.
2. Add the chopped onions and sauté until golden brown.
3. Add the minced garlic and grated ginger to the pan and cook for another minute, stirring constantly.
4. Reduce the heat to low and add the ground cumin, ground coriander, turmeric powder, paprika, and garam masala. Stir well to combine and cook for a couple of minutes to toast the spices.
5. Add the diced tomatoes and cook for about 5 minutes, stirring occasionally.

6. Add the cooked chickpeas to the pan and mix well to coat them with the spice mixture.
7. Pour in the water or vegetable broth, stirring to combine. Cover the pan and simmer the curry for about 15-20 minutes to allow the flavours to meld together. If needed, add more water to adjust the consistency of the curry.
8. Taste and adjust the seasoning with salt as needed.
9. Garnish with fresh coriander leaves and serve hot with steamed rice or naan bread. Squeeze a little fresh lemon juice over the curry for added brightness, if desired.

Saag Aloo

Saag Aloo is a popular North Indian dish made with spinach (saag) and potatoes (aloo). It's a flavourful and comforting dish that is perfect as a side or main course.

Ingredients

- 3 cups spinach leaves, washed and chopped
- 3 medium-sized potatoes, peeled and cubed
- 1 onion, finely chopped
- 2 tomatoes, finely chopped
- 2 green chillies, slit (adjust to taste)
- 3 cloves of garlic, minced
- 1-inch piece of ginger, grated
- 1 teaspoon cumin seeds
- 1 teaspoon turmeric powder
- 1 teaspoon coriander powder
- 1/2 teaspoon red chilli powder (adjust to taste)
- 1/2 teaspoon garam masala
- Salt to taste
- 2 tablespoons oil or ghee
- Fresh coriander leaves, for garnish

Instructions

1. Heat oil or ghee in a large pan or kadai over medium heat. Add the cumin seeds and let them splutter.
2. Add the chopped onions to the pan and sauté until they turn golden brown.
3. Add the minced garlic, grated ginger, and slit green chillies to the pan. Cook for another minute until the raw smell disappears.
4. Stir in the turmeric powder, coriander powder, and red chilli powder. Mix well to combine the spices with the onion mixture.
5. Add the chopped tomatoes to the pan and cook for a few minutes until they become soft and mushy.

6. Add the cubed potatoes to the pan and mix well, ensuring the potatoes are coated with the spices. Cook for a few minutes until the potatoes are slightly browned.
7. Add the chopped spinach to the pan. Stir well to combine the spinach with the potatoes and spices. The spinach will wilt down as it cooks.
8. Reduce the heat to low, cover the pan, and let the saag aloo simmer for about 15-20 minutes, or until the potatoes are cooked through and tender. Stir occasionally to prevent sticking.
9. Add the garam masala and season with salt to taste. Mix well.
10. Garnish the saag aloo with fresh coriander leaves.

Aloo Gobi

Gobi Aloo, also known as Cauliflower Potato Curry, is a popular vegetarian dish in Indian cuisine. It combines tender cauliflower florets and potatoes with a blend of aromatic spices.

Ingredients

- 1 medium-sized cauliflower, cut into florets
- 2 medium-sized potatoes, peeled and cubed
- 1 onion, finely chopped
- 2 tomatoes, finely chopped
- 2 green chillies, slit (adjust to taste)
- 3 cloves of garlic, minced
- 1-inch piece of ginger, grated
- 1 teaspoon cumin seeds
- 1 teaspoon turmeric powder
- 1 teaspoon coriander powder
- 1/2 teaspoon red chilli powder (adjust to taste)
- 1/2 teaspoon garam masala
- Salt to taste
- 2 tablespoons oil or ghee
- Fresh coriander leaves, for garnish

Instructions

1. Heat oil or ghee in a large pan or kadai over medium heat. Add the cumin seeds and let them splutter.
2. Add the chopped onions to the pan and sauté until they turn golden brown.
3. Add the minced garlic, grated ginger, and slit green chillies to the pan. Cook for another minute until the raw smell disappears.
4. Stir in the turmeric powder, coriander powder, and red chilli powder. Mix well to combine the spices with the onion mixture.
5. Add the chopped tomatoes to the pan and cook for a few minutes until they become soft and mushy.

6. Add the cubed potatoes to the pan and mix well, ensuring the potatoes are coated with the spices. Cook for a few minutes until the potatoes are slightly browned.
7. Add the cauliflower florets to the pan. Stir well to combine the cauliflower with the potatoes and spices.
8. Reduce the heat to low, cover the pan, and let the Gobi Aloo simmer for about 15-20 minutes, or until the vegetables are cooked through and tender. Stir occasionally to prevent sticking.
9. Add the garam masala and season with salt to taste. Mix well.
10. Garnish the Gobi Aloo with fresh coriander leaves.

Palak Paneer

Palak Paneer is a popular vegetarian dish from North Indian cuisine. It features soft cubes of paneer (Indian cottage cheese) cooked in a creamy spinach gravy.

Ingredients

- 250 grams paneer, cut into cubes
- 2 bunches of spinach, washed and chopped
- 1 onion, finely chopped
- 2 tomatoes, finely chopped
- 2 green chillies, slit (adjust to taste)
- 3 cloves of garlic, minced
- 1-inch piece of ginger, grated
- 1 teaspoon cumin seeds
- 1 teaspoon garam masala
- 1/2 teaspoon turmeric powder
- 1/2 teaspoon red chilli powder (adjust to taste)
- 1/4 cup fresh cream (optional)
- Salt to taste
- 2 tablespoons oil or ghee

Instructions

1. Heat oil or ghee in a pan over medium heat. Add the cumin seeds and let them splutter.
2. Add the chopped onions to the pan and sauté until they turn golden brown.
3. Add the minced garlic, grated ginger, and slit green chillies to the pan. Cook for another minute until the raw smell disappears.
4. Add the chopped tomatoes to the pan and cook until they become soft and mushy.
5. Add the turmeric powder, red chilli powder, and garam masala to the pan. Mix well to combine the spices with the tomato-onion mixture.

6. Add the chopped spinach to the pan. Stir well to combine the spinach with the spices. The spinach will wilt down as it cooks.
7. Cover the pan and let the spinach cook for about 5-7 minutes on low heat until it is completely wilted.
8. Allow the spinach mixture to cool slightly, then transfer it to a blender or food processor. Blend until you get a smooth puree. If needed, you can add a little water to adjust the consistency.
9. Return the spinach puree to the pan and heat it over medium heat. Add salt to taste and mix well.
10. Add the paneer cubes to the pan and gently stir to coat them with the spinach gravy. Let it simmer for a few minutes until the paneer is heated through.
11. If desired, you can add fresh cream to the dish for added richness. Mix well and cook for another minute.
12. Remove the pan from heat and garnish the Palak Paneer with a drizzle of fresh cream (optional).

Bombay Potatoes

Bombay Potatoes, also known as Bombay Aloo, is a popular Indian dish that features tender potatoes cooked with a blend of aromatic spices. It is a flavourful and comforting side dish that pairs well with rice, roti, or naan bread.

Ingredients

- 4 medium-sized potatoes, peeled and cubed
- 2 tablespoons vegetable oil
- 1 teaspoon mustard seeds
- 1 teaspoon cumin seed
- 1 onion, finely chopped
- 2 green chillies, slit lengthwise
- 1 teaspoon ginger-garlic paste
- 1/2 teaspoon turmeric powder
- 1 teaspoon red chilli powder (adjust according to spice preference)
- 1 teaspoon ground coriander
- 1 teaspoon ground cumin
- 1 teaspoon garam masala
- Salt to taste
- Fresh coriander leaves for garnish

Instructions

1. Heat vegetable oil in a pan or skillet over medium heat. Add mustard seeds and cumin seeds and let them splutter.
2. Add the finely chopped onion and slit green chillies to the pan. Sauté until the onions turn golden brown.
3. Add ginger-garlic paste to the pan and cook for a minute until the raw smell disappears.
4. Add turmeric powder, red chilli powder, ground coriander, ground cumin, and garam masala to the pan. Stir well to combine the spices with the onion mixture.
5. Add the cubed potatoes to the pan and mix well to coat them evenly with the spices. Season with salt to taste.

6. Reduce the heat to low, cover the pan, and let the potatoes cook for about 15-20 minutes, or until they are tender. Stir occasionally to prevent sticking and ensure even cooking.
7. Once the potatoes are cooked through and coated with the spice mixture, remove the pan from heat.
8. Garnish with fresh coriander leaves.
9. Serve the hot and flavourful Bombay flavours as a side dish with rice, roti, or naan bread.

Dhal Makhani

Dal Makhani is a rich and creamy lentil dish that is popular in Indian cuisine. It is made with black lentils (urad dal) and kidney beans (rajma) cooked together with aromatic spices and finished with a touch of cream and butter.

Ingredients

- 1 cup black lentils (whole urad dal)
- 1/4 cup kidney beans (rajma)
- 4 cups water
- 2 tablespoons ghee or butter
- 1 medium-sized onion, finely chopped
- 2 teaspoons ginger-garlic paste
- 2 green chillies, slit lengthwise
- 2 tomatoes, pureed
- 1 teaspoon cumin seeds
- 1/2 teaspoon turmeric powder
- 1 teaspoon red chilli powder
- 1 teaspoon garam masala powder
- 1 teaspoon coriander powder
- Salt to taste
- 1/4 cup fresh cream
- 2 tablespoons chopped fresh coriander leaves for garnish

Instructions

1. Rinse the black lentils and kidney beans thoroughly under running water. Soak them together in enough water for at least 6 hours or overnight. Drain the water before cooking.
2. In a pressure cooker, add the soaked lentils and kidney beans along with 4 cups of water. Close the lid and pressure cook for about 8-10 whistles, or until the lentils and beans are tender and easily mashed. If you don't have a pressure cooker, you can cook them in a pot on the stovetop, but it will take longer.

3. Heat ghee or butter in a separate pan over medium heat. Add the chopped onions and sauté until they turn golden brown.
4. Add the ginger-garlic paste and green chillies to the pan. Cook for a minute until the raw smell disappears.
5. Add the tomato puree to the pan and cook until the oil separates from the mixture.
6. Add cumin seeds, turmeric powder, red chilli powder, garam masala powder, coriander powder, and salt to the pan. Stir well to combine the spices with the onion and tomato mixture.
7. Pour the cooked lentils and kidney beans (along with their cooking liquid) into the pan. Mix well to combine the ingredients.
8. Simmer the dal on low heat for about 20-30 minutes, stirring occasionally, until it thickens and the flavours meld together.
9. Mash some of the lentils and kidney beans with the back of a spoon or a masher to thicken the dal further.
10. Stir in the fresh cream and let the dal simmer for another 5 minutes.
11. Garnish with chopped fresh coriander leaves.
12. Serve hot with steamed rice, naan bread, or roti.

Dal Makhani is a comforting and indulgent dish that is best enjoyed with rice or bread. The creamy texture and aromatic flavours make it a favourite in Indian cuisine.

Chutneys
&
Pickles

Coriander Chutney

Coriander chutney is a flavourful and versatile condiment and pairs well with snacks like samosas, pakoras, or as a spread in sandwiches.

Ingredients

- 2 cups fresh coriander leaves (coriander)
- 1/2 cup fresh mint leaves (optional)
- 1-2 green chillies, chopped (adjust according to spice preference)
- 1 small onion, roughly chopped
- 2 cloves of garlic
- 1-inch piece of ginger, peeled and roughly chopped
- 1 tablespoon lemon juice
- 1 tablespoon roasted cumin powder
- Salt to taste
- Water (as needed)

Instructions

1. Wash the coriander leaves and mint leaves (if using) thoroughly under running water to remove any dirt or impurities. Pat them dry with a clean kitchen towel.
2. In a blender or food processor, add the coriander leaves, mint leaves, chopped green chillies, onion, garlic, and ginger.
3. Blend the ingredients until they form a coarse paste. You may need to scrape down the sides of the blender or add a little water to facilitate the blending process.
4. Add the lemon juice, roasted cumin powder, and salt to the chutney. Blend again until all the ingredients are well combined and the chutney reaches your desired consistency.
5. Taste the chutney and adjust the seasoning, adding more salt or lemon juice if needed.
6. If the chutney is too thick, you can add a little water to thin it out. Add water gradually, blending in between, until you achieve the desired consistency.
7. Store in the refrigerator for up to a week.

Tamarind chutney

Tamarind chutney, also known as Imli chutney, is a popular sweet and tangy condiment and commonly served with chaat snacks, samosas, or used as a dipping sauce.

Ingredients

- 1 cup tamarind pulp
- 1 cup jaggery or brown sugar
- 1 teaspoon roasted cumin powder
- 1 teaspoon red chilli powder
- 1 teaspoon dry ginger powder (saunth)
- 1/2 teaspoon black salt
- 1/2 teaspoon salt
- 1 cup water
- Optional: 1/2 teaspoon chaat masala (for added flavour)

Instructions

1. In a saucepan, combine the tamarind pulp and water. Bring it to a boil over medium heat, then reduce the heat and let it simmer for about 5 minutes to soften the tamarind.
2. Remove the saucepan from heat and allow the tamarind mixture to cool down slightly.
3. Once cooled, strain the tamarind pulp through a fine-mesh sieve into another saucepan or bowl. Use the back of a spoon or spatula to press and extract as much pulp as possible. Discard any solids or fibers left behind.
4. Place the strained tamarind pulp back on the stovetop over medium heat. Add the jaggery or brown sugar and stir until it dissolves completely.
5. Add the roasted cumin powder, red chilli powder, dry ginger powder, black salt, and salt to the tamarind mixture. Stir well to combine all the ingredients.

6. Allow the mixture to simmer for about 10-15 minutes, stirring occasionally, until it thickens to a syrupy consistency. Keep in mind that the chutney will thicken further as it cools, so it's okay if it appears slightly runny.
7. Remove the saucepan from heat and let the tamarind chutney cool down completely. As it cools, it will continue to thicken.
8. Optional If desired, you can add chaat masala to enhance the flavour of the chutney. Stir it in during the cooling process.
9. Once cooled, transfer the tamarind chutney to a clean, airtight jar or container. It can be stored in the refrigerator for up to a month.

Tamarind chutney is now ready to be enjoyed! Serve it with your favourite chaat snacks, samosas, or use it as a dipping sauce. Its sweet and tangy flavour will add a delightful kick to your dishes.

Garlic Chutney

Ingredients

- 1 cup peeled garlic cloves
- 6-8 dried red chillies (adjust according to spice preference)
- 1 teaspoon cumin seeds
- 1 teaspoon coriander seeds
- 1 tablespoon sesame seeds
- 1 tablespoon oil
- 1 tablespoon tamarind paste or lemon juice
- Salt to taste
- Water (as needed)

Instructions

1. Heat a small pan over low heat and dry roast the dried red chillies, cumin seeds, coriander seeds, and sesame seeds for a few minutes until they become fragrant. Be careful not to burn them.
2. Transfer the roasted ingredients to a blender or food processor.
3. In the same pan, heat the oil over medium heat. Add the peeled garlic cloves and sauté them until they turn golden brown. Make sure to stir continuously to avoid burning.
4. Add the sautéed garlic cloves to the blender or food processor along with the roasted spices.
5. Add the tamarind paste or lemon juice, salt, and a little water to the blender. Blend all the ingredients together until you achieve a smooth and thick paste. If needed, add more water gradually to adjust the consistency.
6. Taste the chutney and adjust the seasoning, adding more salt or lemon juice if desired.
7. Transfer the garlic chutney to a clean, airtight jar or container. It can be stored in the refrigerator for up to a week.

Date Chutney

Date chutney, also known as Khajur chutney, is a sweet and tangy condiment commonly used in Indian cuisine. It is a popular accompaniment for snacks like samosas, pakoras, or as a spread in sandwiches.

Ingredients

- 1 cup pitted dates, chopped
- 1/2 cup tamarind pulp
- 1/4 cup jaggery or brown sugar
- 1 teaspoon roasted cumin powder
- 1/2 teaspoon red chilli powder (adjust to taste)
- 1/2 teaspoon ginger powder (saunth)
- 1/2 teaspoon black salt
- 1/2 teaspoon salt
- 1 cup water

Instructions

1. In a saucepan, combine the chopped dates, tamarind pulp, jaggery or brown sugar, and water. Stir well to combine.
2. Place the saucepan over medium heat and bring the mixture to a boil. Once boiling, reduce the heat to low and let it simmer for about 10-15 minutes, stirring occasionally, until the dates soften and the mixture thickens.
3. Remove the saucepan from heat and allow the mixture to cool down slightly.
4. Transfer the mixture to a blender or food processor and blend until smooth. You can adjust the consistency by adding a little more water if desired.
5. Pour the blended mixture back into the saucepan and place it over low heat.
6. Add the roasted cumin powder, red chilli powder, ginger powder, black salt, and salt to the chutney. Stir well to combine all the ingredients.

7. Let the chutney simmer for another 5-10 minutes, stirring occasionally, to allow the flavours to meld together and the chutney to thicken further.
8. Remove the saucepan from heat and let the date chutney cool down completely.
9. Once cooled, transfer the chutney to a clean, airtight jar or container. It can be stored in the refrigerator for up to a month.

Lime Pickle

Ingredients

- 8-10 limes
- 3-4 tablespoons salt
- 2 tablespoons mustard seeds
- 1 tablespoon fenugreek seeds
- 1 tablespoon turmeric powder
- 1 tablespoon red chili powder
- 1 tablespoon fennel seeds
- 1 tablespoon nigella seeds (kalonji)
- 1 cup vegetable oil

Instructions

1. Wash and cut each lime into small pieces or wedge.
2. In a bowl, combine the lime pieces with salt. Mix well, ensuring all the pieces are coated with salt. Set it aside for 1-2 days, allowing the salt to draw out moisture from the limes.
3. After 1-2 days, heat a dry pan over medium heat. Add mustard seeds and fenugreek seeds to the pan. Dry roast them until they start to release their aroma and turn slightly darker in color. Remove from heat and let them cool.
4. Grind the roasted mustard seeds and fenugreek seeds into a coarse powder using a spice grinder or mortar and pestle.
5. In a separate bowl, combine the powdered mustard and fenugreek seeds with turmeric powder, red chili powder, fennel seeds, and nigella seeds. Mix well to create a spice blend.
6. Heat the vegetable oil in a pan over medium heat. Once hot, add the spice blend and sauté for a minute or until fragrant.
7. Add the salted lime pieces to the pan and stir to coat them evenly with the spice mixture. Cook for about 5 minutes, stirring occasionally.
8. Remove the pan from heat and let the pickle cool completely. Transfer it to a clean, sterilized glass jar.

Mango Pickle

Ingredients

- 2 large raw green mangoes
- 4 tablespoons salt
- 2 tablespoons mustard seeds
- 1 tablespoon fenugreek seeds
- 1 tablespoon fennel seeds
- 1 tablespoon nigella seeds (kalonji)
- 1 tablespoon turmeric powder
- 2 tablespoons red chili powder
- 1/2 cup mustard oil (or any vegetable oil)
- 4-5 cloves garlic, finely chopped

Instructions

1. Wash the mangoes thoroughly and pat them dry. Cut them into small pieces, discarding the seed.
2. In a bowl, add the mango pieces and salt. Mix well, ensuring all the pieces are coated with salt. Set it aside for 4-5 hours or overnight, allowing the salt to draw out moisture from the mangoes.
3. After the resting time, heat a dry pan over medium heat. Add mustard seeds, fenugreek seeds, fennel seeds, and nigella seeds to the pan. Dry roast them until they start to release their aroma and turn slightly darker in color. Remove from heat and let them cool.
4. Grind the roasted seeds into a coarse powder using a spice grinder or mortar and pestle.
5. In a separate bowl, combine the powdered seeds with turmeric powder, red chili powder, and chopped garlic. Mix well to create a spice blend.
6. Heat the mustard oil in a pan over medium heat until it reaches its smoking point. Turn off the heat and let the oil cool for a few minutes.
7. Once the oil has cooled slightly, add the spice blend to the pan and mix well. The oil should sizzle when the spices are added.

8. Add the salted mango pieces to the pan and toss them in the spice-infused oil until they are well coated.
9. Transfer the mango pickle mixture to a clean, sterilized glass jar. Press it down firmly to remove any air bubbles and ensure the mango pieces are submerged in the oil.
10. Allow the pickle to mature in a cool, dry place for at least a week before consuming. During this time, the flavours will develop and the mango pieces will soften.

Kachumba Salad

Ingredients

- 1 cucumber, finely chopped
- 1 tomato, finely chopped
- 1 onion, finely chopped
- 1 green chilli, finely chopped (optional, adjust to taste)
- 1 small carrot, grated
- 1 tablespoon chopped fresh coriander leaves
- Juice of 1 lemon
- 1/2 teaspoon roasted cumin powder
- Salt to taste

Instructions

1. In a mixing bowl, combine the finely chopped cucumber, tomato, onion, green chilli (if using), grated carrot, and chopped coriander leaves.
2. In a small bowl, whisk together the lemon juice, roasted cumin powder, and salt.
3. Pour the dressing over the chopped vegetables in the mixing bowl.
4. Toss the ingredients well to coat the vegetables evenly with the dressing. Make sure all the vegetables are well combined.
5. Taste the salad and adjust the seasoning, adding more salt or lemon juice if needed.
6. Let the Kachumba salad sit for about 10-15 minutes before serving. This allows the flavours to meld together and the vegetables to marinate in the dressing.
7. Give the salad a final toss before serving to ensure that the dressing is evenly distributed.
8. Serve the Kachumba salad as a refreshing side dish with your favourite Indian dishes or as a standalone salad.

Raita

Raita is a refreshing and cooling yogurt-based side dish that complements spicy Indian curries and biryanis. It's a perfect accompaniment to balance the heat and add a burst of flavour to your meal.

Ingredients

- 2 cups plain yogurt
- 1 cucumber, peeled and finely chopped
- 1 medium-sized tomato, finely chopped
- 1/4 cup finely chopped red onion (optional)
- 2 tablespoons fresh coriander leaves, chopped
- 1/2 teaspoon roasted cumin powder
- 1/4 teaspoon black salt (kala namak) or regular salt, or to taste
- A pinch of black pepper powder (optional)
- A pinch of red chilli powder (optional)

Instructions

1. In a mixing bowl, whisk the yogurt until smooth and creamy.
2. Add the chopped cucumber, tomato, red onion (if using), and fresh coriander leaves to the yogurt. Mix well to combine.
3. Sprinkle roasted cumin powder, black salt, black pepper powder (if using), and red chilli powder (if using) over the raita. Stir well to incorporate the spices.
4. Taste and adjust the seasoning if needed, adding more salt or spices according to your preference.
5. Cover the bowl and refrigerate the raita for at least 30 minutes to allow the flavours to meld together and chill.
6. Before serving, give the raita a final stir. If desired, you can garnish it with a sprinkle of roasted cumin powder and fresh coriander leaves.

Desserts

· ·

Dhokla

For the dhokla batter

- 1 cup gram flour (besan)
- 1/4 cup semolina (sooji)
- 1/4 cup yogurt (plain curd)
- 1 teaspoon ginger paste
- 1 teaspoon green chilli paste
- 1/2 teaspoon turmeric powder
- 1/2 teaspoon salt, or to taste
- 1 teaspoon sugar
- 1 teaspoon lemon juice
- 1 teaspoon fruit salt (eno)
- 1 tablespoon oil

For the tempering

- 2 tablespoons oil
- 1 teaspoon mustard seeds
- 1 teaspoon sesame seeds
- 1 tablespoon chopped curry leaves
- 2 green chillies, slit lengthwise
- 1/4 cup water
- 1 tablespoon sugar
- 2 tablespoons lemon juice
- Fresh coriander leaves for garnish
- Grated coconut for garnish (optional)

Instructions

1. In a mixing bowl, combine gram flour, semolina, yogurt, ginger paste, green chilli paste, turmeric powder, salt, sugar, lemon juice, and oil. Mix well to form a smooth batter. Add water as needed to achieve a pourable consistency.
2. Grease a steamer plate or a baking dish with oil. Set it aside.
3. In a large pot or steamer, bring water to a boil.

4. Just before steaming, add fruit salt (eno) to the batter and mix gently. The batter will become frothy.
5. Pour the batter into the greased steamer plate or baking dish, spreading it evenly.
6. Place the plate or dish in the steamer and cover it with a lid. Steam on medium heat for about 15-20 minutes, or until a toothpick inserted into the dhokla comes out clean.
7. Once the dhokla is steamed, remove it from the steamer and let it cool for a few minutes.
8. Cut the dhokla into desired shapes, such as squares or diamonds.
9. For tempering, heat oil in a small pan. Add mustard seeds and let them splutter. Then add sesame seeds, chopped curry leaves, and slit green chillies. Sauté for a few seconds.
10. Add water, sugar, and lemon juice to the pan. Stir well and let the mixture come to a boil.
11. Pour the tempering mixture over the steamed dhokla, ensuring it is evenly distributed.
12. Garnish the dhokla with fresh coriander leaves and grated coconut (if using).
13. Allow the dhokla to absorb the tempering flavours for a few minutes before serving.
14. Serve the dhokla warm or at room temperature as a snack or appetizer. It can be enjoyed on its own or with green chutney or tamarind chutney.

Gulab Jamun

One of the most beloved and iconic Indian desserts is gulab Jamun. These sweet, syrup-soaked dumplings are made from a mixture of khoya (reduced milk solids) and flour, deep-fried until golden brown, and then soaked in a fragrant sugar syrup.

For the Gulab Jamun

- 1 cup khoya (milk solids)
- 1/4 cup all-purpose flour
- 1/4 teaspoon baking powder
- 2 tablespoons ghee (clarified butter)
- A pinch of cardamom powder
- A pinch of saffron strands (optional)
- Chopped nuts (such as pistachios or almonds) for garnish
- Oil or ghee for deep frying

For the Sugar Syrup

- 2 cups sugar
- 2 cups water
- A few strands of saffron
- 1/2 teaspoon cardamom powder
- 1 teaspoon rose water

Instructions

1. In a mixing bowl, crumble the khoya and add the all-purpose flour, baking powder, cardamom powder, and saffron strands (if using). Mix well to combine the ingredients.
2. Add the ghee to the mixture and knead it into a smooth and soft dough. If the dough feels dry, you can add a little milk or water to moisten it.
3. Divide the dough into small portions and roll each portion into a smooth ball, ensuring there are no cracks on the surface. Make sure

the balls are small, as they will expand slightly when fried and soaked in syrup.

4. Heat oil or ghee in a deep pan or kadai for deep frying. The oil should be medium hot, around 180°C (350°F).

5. Gently slide a few dough balls into the hot oil and fry them on medium heat until they turn golden brown. Make sure to stir them gently in the oil for even cooking.

6. Once fried, remove the Gulab Jamuns from the oil and drain them on a kitchen paper towel to remove excess oil.

7. In the meantime, prepare the sugar syrup. In a separate pan, combine the sugar and water and bring it to a boil. Stir until the sugar is completely dissolved.

8. Add the saffron strands and cardamom powder to the syrup. Let the syrup simmer for about 5 minutes until it slightly thickens.

9. Remove the syrup from heat and add the rose water. Stir well to combine.

10. Gently drop the fried Gulab Jamuns into the warm syrup and let them soak for at least 30 minutes to an hour. The longer they soak, the softer and more flavourful they become.

11. Serve the Gulab Jamuns warm or at room temperature, garnished with chopped nuts.

Ras Malai

Ras Malai is a delectable Indian dessert made with soft, spongy cottage cheese dumplings soaked in sweetened, thickened milk flavoured with cardamom and garnished with nuts.

For the Ras Malai dumplings

- 2 cups full-fat milk
- 1 tablespoon lemon juice or vinegar
- 1/4 cup all-purpose flour
- 1/4 teaspoon baking powder
- A pinch of cardamom powder
- A few strands of saffron
- Chopped nuts (such as pistachios or almonds) for garnish

For the sweetened milk

- 4 cups full-fat milk
- 1 cup sugar
- A pinch of cardamom powder
- A few strands of saffron

Instructions

1. In a large saucepan, bring 2 cups of milk to a gentle boil. As the milk starts boiling, add lemon juice or vinegar gradually while stirring continuously. The milk will curdle and separate into solids (paneer) and whey.
2. Line a fine-mesh strainer or cheesecloth over a bowl and strain the curdled milk to separate the solids. Rinse the paneer under cold water to remove any lemony taste.
3. Squeeze out the excess water from the paneer and transfer it to a clean, dry surface. Knead the paneer for a few minutes until it becomes smooth and pliable.

4. In a mixing bowl, combine the paneer, all-purpose flour, baking powder, and cardamom powder. Knead the mixture gently until it forms a soft dough.
5. Divide the dough into small portions and roll each portion into a smooth ball. Press each ball gently to flatten it slightly.
6. In a separate wide pan, bring 4 cups of milk to a boil. Stir occasionally to prevent the milk from scorching.
7. Add the sugar, cardamom powder, and saffron strands to the boiling milk. Stir well to dissolve the sugar.
8. Gently slide the paneer balls into the boiling milk and let them cook on low heat for about 10-12 minutes. The dumplings will increase in size and become spongy.
9. Once cooked, remove the pan from heat and allow the Ras Malai to cool to room temperature. The dumplings will absorb more milk and become softer as they cool.
10. Refrigerate the Ras Malai for a few hours to chill and set.
11. Garnish the chilled Ras Malai with chopped nuts and saffron strands before serving.

Coconut Barfi

Coconut Barfi, also known as Nariyal Barfi, is a delicious and popular Indian sweet made with grated coconut, sugar, and flavoured with cardamom.

Ingredients

- 2 cups grated coconut (fresh or desiccated)
- 1 cup condensed milk
- 1/2 cup sugar
- 1/2 teaspoon cardamom powder
- A pinch of saffron strands (optional)
- Chopped nuts (such as almonds or pistachios) for garnish

Instructions

1. Heat a non-stick pan or a heavy-bottomed pan on medium heat.
2. Add the grated coconut to the pan and sauté for a few minutes until it releases its aroma and turns slightly golden. This step helps to remove any moisture from the coconut.
3. Reduce the heat to low and add the condensed milk to the pan. Mix well to combine the coconut and condensed milk.
4. Add the sugar to the mixture and stir continuously to prevent sticking or burning.
5. Cook the mixture on low heat, stirring frequently, until it thickens and starts to leave the sides of the pan. This may take around 15-20 minutes.
6. Once the mixture thickens, add the cardamom powder and saffron strands (if using). Mix well to incorporate the flavours.
7. Grease a square or rectangular baking tray or plate with ghee or butter.
8. Transfer the cooked coconut mixture to the greased tray and spread it evenly using a spatula or the back of a spoon.
9. Garnish the top with chopped nuts, pressing them lightly into the surface.

10. Allow the Coconut Barfi to cool completely at room temperature. Once cooled, refrigerate for a couple of hours to set.
11. Once set, cut the Coconut Barfi into desired shapes, such as squares or diamonds.

Coconut Barfi is now ready to be enjoyed! Store the Barfi in an airtight container in the refrigerator to maintain its freshness.

Rice Pudding

Indian rice pudding, also known as kheer, is a creamy and sweet dessert made with rice, milk, sugar, and flavoured with cardamom and nuts. It is a popular and comforting dessert in Indian cuisine.

Ingredients

- 1/2 cup basmati rice
- 4 cups whole milk
- 1/2 cup sugar (adjust according to sweetness preference)
- 1/2 teaspoon cardamom powder
- 2 tablespoons chopped nuts (such as almonds, cashews, or pistachios)
- 1 tablespoon raisins (optional)
- Saffron strands (a pinch) soaked in 1 tablespoon warm milk (optional)
- 1 tablespoon ghee (clarified butter)
- Chopped nuts and saffron strands for garnish

Instructions

1. Rinse the basmati rice under running water until the water runs clear. Soak the rice in water for 30 minutes, then drain and set aside.
2. Heat ghee in a heavy-bottomed pan or pot over medium heat. Add the soaked and drained rice and sauté for a couple of minutes until the rice turns slightly translucent.
3. Add the whole milk to the pan with the rice and bring it to a boil. Reduce the heat to low and let the rice simmer, stirring occasionally to prevent sticking, for about 30-35 minutes or until the rice is cooked and the milk has thickened.
4. Add the sugar and mix well until it dissolves completely. Continue to simmer for another 5-10 minutes until the mixture reaches a desired thick consistency.
5. Add the cardamom powder, chopped nuts, raisins (if using), and saffron-soaked milk (if using). Mix well to combine all the flavours.

6. Remove the pan from heat and let the rice pudding cool for a few minutes. It will thicken further as it cools.
7. Serve the rice pudding warm or chilled, garnished with chopped nuts and saffron strands on top.

Indian rice pudding can be enjoyed as a dessert after a meal or as a sweet treat on its own. It can be served warm or chilled, according to personal preference. The creamy texture and aromatic flavours of the kheer make it a delightful and comforting dessert. Enjoy the rich and creamy goodness of Indian rice pudding!

Kulfi

Kulfi is a rich and creamy Indian frozen dessert that is often flavoured with cardamom, saffron, and nuts. It is a popular treat enjoyed during hot summer days.

Ingredients

- 2 cups full-fat milk
- 1/2 cup condensed milk
- 1/4 cup sugar (adjust according to sweetness preference)
- 1/2 teaspoon cardamom powder
- A pinch of saffron strands (optional)
- 2 tablespoons chopped nuts (such as almonds, pistachios, or cashews)
- 1 tablespoon rose water (optional)
- Kulfi molds or small bowls
- Popsicle sticks or wooden skewers

Instructions

1. In a heavy-bottomed saucepan, bring the full-fat milk to a boil over medium heat. Stir occasionally to prevent the milk from scorching.
2. Once the milk comes to a boil, reduce the heat to low and let it simmer. Keep stirring occasionally to avoid forming a skin on the surface.
3. After about 20-25 minutes, the milk will reduce and thicken to approximately half its original volume. It should have a creamy consistency.
4. Add the condensed milk and sugar to the simmering milk. Mix well until the sugar is dissolved completely.
5. Continue to simmer the mixture for another 10-15 minutes, stirring occasionally, until it thickens further and becomes slightly grainy in texture.
6. Add the cardamom powder, saffron strands (if using), and chopped nuts to the mixture. Mix well to distribute the flavours evenly.

7. Remove the pan from heat and let the mixture cool for a few minutes. Stir in the rose water (if using) for a fragrant touch.
8. Pour the kulfi mixture into kulfi molds or small bowls. If using bowls, cover them with aluminium foil and insert a popsicle stick or wooden skewer into each kulfi.
9. Place the kulfi molds or bowls in the freezer and let them freeze for at least 6 hours or overnight until they are completely set.
10. To serve, remove the kulfi from the molds or bowls by running them under warm water for a few seconds. Gently pull out the kulfi using the popsicle stick or skewer.
11. Garnish the kulfi with additional chopped nuts if desired and serve immediately.

Halwa

Ingredients

- 1 cup semolina (rava or sooji)
- 1 cup sugar
- 1/4 cup ghee (clarified butter)
- 1/4 cup chopped nuts (such as almonds, cashews, and pistachios)
- 4 cups water
- 1/2 teaspoon cardamom powder
- A pinch of saffron strands (optional)
- Raisins for garnish (optional)

Instructions

1. Heat the ghee in a large pan or kadai over medium heat.
2. Add the semolina to the pan and roast it in the ghee until it turns golden brown and releases a nutty aroma. Stir continuously to ensure even browning and to prevent burning. This should take about 8-10 minutes.
3. In a separate pot, bring 4 cups of water to a boil.
4. Slowly and carefully pour the boiling water into the roasted semolina while stirring continuously. Be cautious as the mixture may splutter.
5. Cook the semolina in the water, stirring constantly, until it absorbs the water and thickens. This should take about 3-4 minutes.
6. Add the sugar to the pan and continue stirring until the sugar dissolves completely.
7. Reduce the heat to low and continue to cook the mixture, stirring frequently, until it thickens further and starts to leave the sides of the pan. This process will take about 5-6 minutes.
8. Add the cardamom powder and saffron strands (if using), and mix well.
9. In a separate small pan, heat a little ghee and roast the chopped nuts until they turn golden brown. Remove from heat and set aside.
10. Remove the halwa from the heat and transfer it to a serving dish. Garnish with the roasted nuts and optional raisins.

Milk Barfi

Ingredients

- 2 cups milk powder
- 1 cup condensed milk
- 1/4 cup ghee (clarified butter)
- 1/4 cup milk
- 1/2 teaspoon cardamom powder
- Chopped nuts for garnish (such as almonds, cashews, and pistachios)
- Edible silver foil (varak) for decoration (optional)

Instructions

1. Heat the ghee in a non-stick pan over medium heat.
2. Add the milk powder to the pan and sauté it in the ghee for 2-3 minutes, stirring continuously to prevent burning. The milk powder will start to release a pleasant aroma.
3. Reduce the heat to low and add the condensed milk to the pan. Mix well to combine the milk powder and condensed milk.
4. Gradually pour in the milk while stirring continuously. This will help to create a smooth and creamy consistency.
5. Cook the mixture on low heat, stirring constantly, until it thickens and starts to leave the sides of the pan. This should take about 8-10 minutes.
6. Add the cardamom powder to the pan and mix well to incorporate the flavour.
7. Remove the pan from heat and transfer the mixture to a greased plate or tray. Use the back of a spoon or a spatula to spread the mixture evenly and smoothen the surface.
8. Sprinkle the chopped nuts over the surface of the barfi and gently press them into the mixture.
9. Allow the barfi to cool completely and set at room temperature for a few hours. You can also refrigerate it for faster setting.
10. Once the barfi has set, cut it into square or diamond-shaped pieces.

Drinks

Mango Lassi

Ingredients

- 1 ripe mango
- 1 cup plain yogurt
- 1/2 cup milk
- 2 tablespoons sugar (adjust according to your preference)
- A pinch of ground cardamom (optional)
- Ice cubes (optional)

Instructions

1. Peel and dice the ripe mango, discarding the seed and skin.
2. In a blender, add the diced mango, yogurt, milk, sugar, and cardamom (if using).
3. Blend the ingredients until smooth and creamy. If desired, you can add a few ice cubes to make it colder and thicker.
4. Taste the lassi and adjust the sweetness by adding more sugar if needed. Blend again briefly to incorporate.
5. Pour the mango lassi into serving glasses.
6. You can garnish the lassi with a sprinkle of ground cardamom or a few strands of saffron for added aroma and presentation.
7. Serve chilled and enjoy!

Feel free to adjust the sweetness and consistency of the lassi according to your taste preferences. You can also experiment by adding a dash of rose water or a squeeze of lime juice for different flavour variations. Enjoy your homemade mango lassi!

Chai Masala

Chai masala is a blend of spices used to flavour and enhance the taste of traditional Indian tea, known as chai.

Ingredients

- 2 cinnamon sticks
- 8-10 green cardamom pods
- 8-10 whole cloves
- 1 teaspoon whole black peppercorns
- 1 teaspoon fennel seeds
- 1 teaspoon ground ginger
- 1/2 teaspoon ground nutmeg (optional)

Instructions

1. In a skillet or pan, dry roast the cinnamon sticks, green cardamom pods, cloves, black peppercorns, and fennel seeds over medium heat for a few minutes until they become fragrant. Stir continuously to prevent burning.
2. Remove the spices from the heat and let them cool down slightly.
3. Once cooled, transfer the roasted spices to a spice grinder or mortar and pestle. Grind them to a fine powder.
4. Add the ground ginger and ground nutmeg (if using) to the spice blend and mix well.
5. Your homemade chai masala is ready!
6. Store the chai masala in an airtight container in a cool, dry place. It can be kept for several months and used whenever you prepare chai.

To use the chai masala, add a pinch or a teaspoon (depending on your preference for spiciness) to your regular tea while brewing. You can adjust the amount of chai masala according to your taste. Enjoy the aromatic and flavourful experience of homemade masala chai!

Nimbu Pani (Lemonade)

Ingredients

- 4 cups water
- Juice of 3-4 lemons
- 1/4 cup sugar (adjust to taste)
- A pinch of salt
- A pinch of roasted cumin powder (optional)
- Ice cubes
- Fresh mint leaves for garnish

Instructions

1. In a pitcher, combine the water, lemon juice, sugar, and salt. Stir well until the sugar dissolves.
2. Taste and adjust the sweetness and tanginess by adding more sugar or lemon juice if desired.
3. Add a pinch of roasted cumin powder for a hint of flavour (optional).
4. Chill the nimbu pani in the refrigerator for at least 30 minutes.
5. Just before serving, add ice cubes to the pitcher and stir.
6. Pour the nimbu pani into glasses, garnish with fresh mint leaves, and serve chilled.

Other Products
&
Publications

Steven Heap Recipes on YouTube

This channel started back in 2016 and now has millions of views and offers over 1400 video recipes to date with new recipes being uploaded regularly as well as travel blogs, restaurant visits and reviews.

Link: https://www.youtube.com/c/stevenheaprecipes

Taste of India Spices

For all your Indian food spice needs visit 'Taste of India Spices' on eBay where you can purchase all your premium quality Whole and Powdered Spices as well as highly popular Spice Blends that are all freshly roasted and ground to order for superior taste and aroma.

Link: ebay.co.uk/usr/toi_spices

Free UK Delivery. Send inquiries for world-wide shipping & enquiries.

About The author

Although Steven Heap is native British his first experience of Indian food was in his family home. His grandfather had served in India towards the end of the Second World War and returned to England with a few recipes he had been given. His grandfather would cook a curry every Friday night which then inspired Steven's mother with her love of Indian food. At the age of 14 he got a part-time job washing up and prepping vegetables at an Indian restaurant where he expanded his food knowledge.

After going away to university in London in the early 2000s he lived at various lodgings including Pakistani and Indian homes where he cooked side by side with the residents. He began to fall in love with the food from South Asia and quickly incorporated it into his daily diet.

After graduating from university he first visited India to further explore his food interests. This was the start of many trips in his quest for food inspiration. In 2008 he moved to Malaysia which has a large Indian community and made regular trips all over Asia including Sri Lanka *and of course* to explore more of the food culture of India.

By this time he had become accomplished in the Indian kitchen and returning to the UK went on to cook at several British restaurants and also offered cookery classes. His creativity was noticed and he was invited to cook for the famous music star Wiz Khalifa and also rock group Paramore on European tours which inspired the confidence to write 2 Indian food books and start a YouTube channel showcasing his dishes. Steven also regularly competes in cookery competitions against industry standard chefs and has never places less then third position, and in 2018 qualified for the World Culinary Cup in Luxembourg representing the UK in the Indian category.

Steven's unique and varied insight into Indian food combined with his passion for spreading the popularity of this cuisine was his goal in writing this book and he has dedicated himself to become a lifelong student of Indian cuisine and wants to inspire others.

Printed in Great Britain
by Amazon

27088266R00084